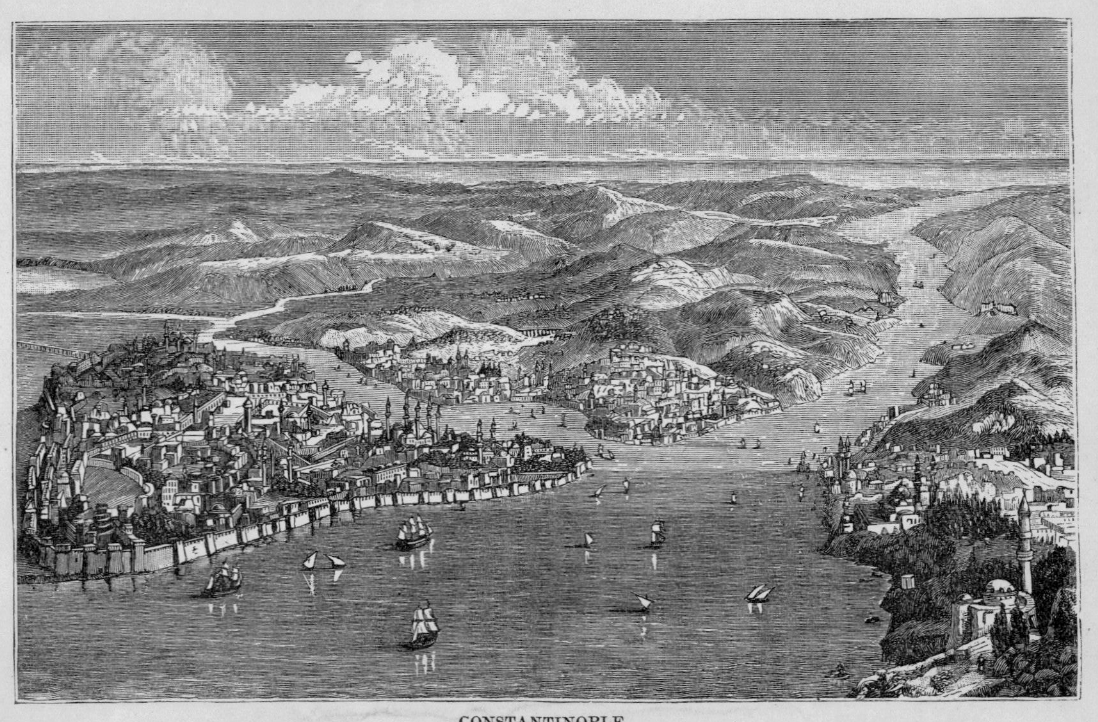

CONSTANTINOPLE.

SHORT HISTORY

OF

THE EARLY CHURCH

BY

JOHN F. HURST, D.D.

AUTHOR OF "SHORT HISTORY OF THE REFORMATION" ETC.

WITH ILLUSTRATIONS

Emblem of the Church—Dove and Sheaf. From a Gem

NEW YORK
CHAUTAUQUA PRESS
C. L. S. C. DEPARTMENT
805 BROADWAY
1886

The required books of the C. L. S. C. are recommended by a Council of six. It must, however, be understood that recommendation does not involve an approval by the Council, or by any member of it, of every principle or doctrine contained in the book recommended.

CONTENTS.

ILLUSTRATIONS.

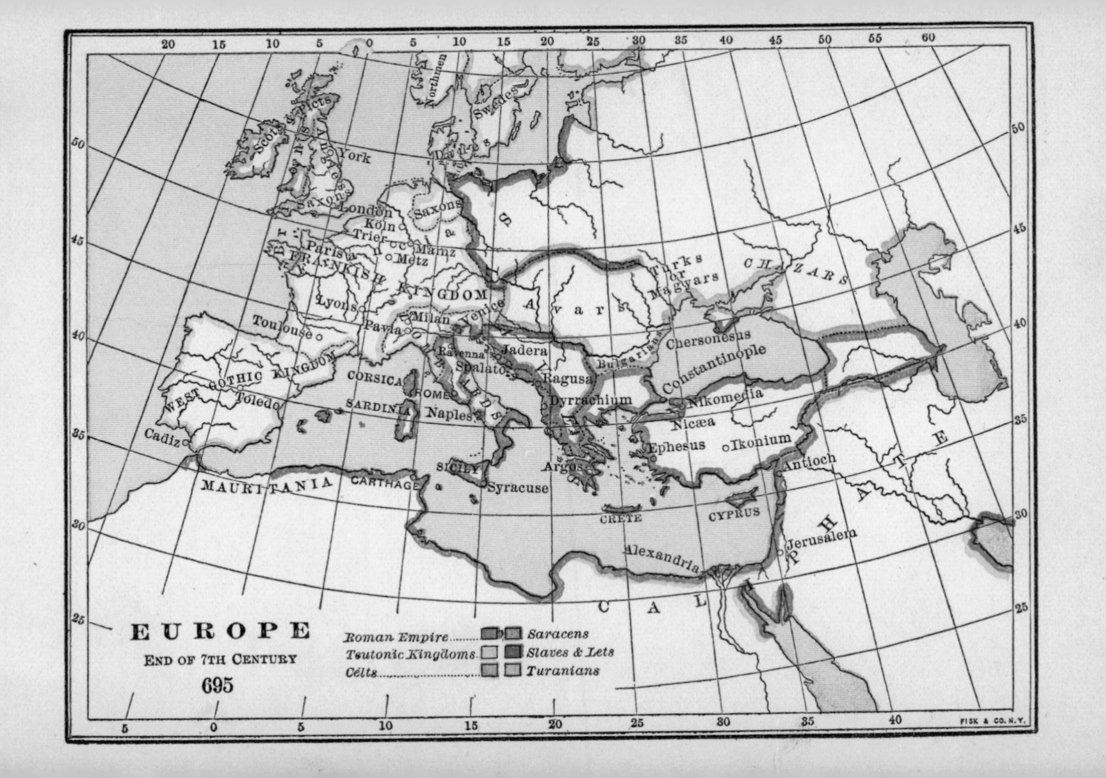
EUROPE
END OF 7TH CENTURY
695
Roman Empire
Teutonic Kingdoms
Celts
Saracens
Slaves & Lets
Turanians
Northmen
Swedes
Danes
Scots
Picts
Angles
York
Saxons
London
Köln
Trier
Mainz
Metz
Paris
FRANKISH KINGDOM
Lyons
Toulouse
Milan
Pavia
Venice
Ravenna
Spalato
Jadera
Ragusa
Dyrrachium
Bulgarians
Turks or Magyars
CHAZARS
Avars
Chersonesus
Constantinople
Nikomedia
Nicæa
Ephesus
Ikonium
Antioch
CALIPHATE
Jerusalem
Alexandria
CYPRUS
CRETE
Argos
Syracuse
SICILY
CARTHAGE
MAURITANIA
SARDINIA
CORSICA
ROME
Naples
WEST GOTHIC KINGDOM
Toledo
Cadiz
FISK & CO. N.Y.

SHORT HISTORY OF THE EARLY CHURCH.

A.D. 30-750.

CHAPTER I.

THE CHURCH AND ITS HISTORY.

1. The History of the Church. The visible Church consists of the organized believers in Christ and the followers of his life. General history reveals the constant presence of a superintending Providence. The rise and fall of nations is not an idle play of human passions. Schiller's aphorism is a just recognition of God's constant watchfulness and justice: "The world's history is the world's judgment." The wild currents have never been permitted to flow on without divine control. When the hour came for the wrong to cease, the controlling hand intervened. The result was always the triumph of the right. In the history of the Church the divine superintendence has been far more prominent. While, in secular history, the spiritual forces lay largely in the background, in the life of the Church they have come out boldly into the clear foreground. Though often in the wrong, and divided in opinions, the Church has been saved from fatal error and downfall by divine interposition. Even when it has been grossly superstitious, and the teacher of false doctrine, God has always raised up true servants, who became the heroes of a holy cause and the heralds of a brighter day. The champion of a wrong cause has always had his plans fail through the work of some brave and pure opponent. There has been an Athanasius to meet every Arius. To counteract a Leo X., there has always arisen a fearless Luther. To show when the divine force has controlled all human events, and made them subserve the steady progress of God's servants, is the mission of the historian of the Church. His task is not to untie a tangled skein, but to follow the golden thread of the divine presence in all the Christian ages.

2. The Completion of Christ's Personal Ministry. When our Lord's passion had occurred, three important works were accomplished. He had communicated his gospel to men, he had set a spotless example before the world, and he had achieved universal redemption by his voluntary death. His subsequent resurrection and ascension were the visible proofs of the truth of his doctrines. They were more than this—they were the twofold assurance to his followers, then and in all later ages, that they who believe in him, and love him, shall enjoy his constant presence during life, and afterwards enter upon the inheritance of heaven. Christ, immediately before his ascension, commanded his disciples to remain in Jerusalem until they should be endued with power from on high. Here lay his promise of spiritual preparation for their ministry. It was, at the same time, a direct lesson that a special spiritual preparation and plenitude were, for all time, a requisite for the successful preaching of the gospel. Without the descent of the Spirit at Pentecost there would have been no impulsive power in Christianity.

3. The Preaching at Pentecost. The Pentecost was the Jewish national thanksgiving day. It was the feast of weeks, or harvest feast-day, which commemorated the gift of the Law to Moses, and at the same time gave occasion to return thanks for the annual products of the soil. Its observance was associated with the most touching memories connected with the founding of the theocracy, and with the subsequent preserving care of a bountiful Creator. Jews in all lands united with their brethren in Palestine in an annual visit to Jerusalem, to celebrate the day. The first Christian Pentecost came on the fiftieth day after our Lord's resurrection and the tenth after his ascension. There were Jews in the sacred city from all parts of the known world. On that day the promise of the Spirit's descent was fulfilled. Cloven tongues of fire flamed above the heads of the disciples. The miraculous gift of utterance was imparted. The multitude of Jews was attracted to the place where the disciples were. Each worshipper, whatever his language, understood the preaching. Peter explained to the people the significance of the scene, and applied the descent of the Spirit to the work of our Lord. The result was the addition of three thousand to the body of believers.

4. **The Organization of the Church** was the direct result of the remarkable scenes at Pentecost. Measures were soon taken for a unifying ecclesiastical polity. Even before Pentecost a new apostle, Matthias, was chosen in place of the fallen Judas. Orders of ministers and lay members were established, for the preaching of the gospel, the care of the needy, and the building up of the body of believers. Only a general organization, however, was effected. The most simple arrangements were made for government, as the believers were as yet but few, and confined to a narrow area.

The more elaborate polity was left for the future needs of the Church, to take its shape according to the expansion of the societies and their individual requirements.

5. The Practical Life of the Christians was at once simple and beautiful. It was a type of all the essential qualities which Christ had taught, as requisite for pure living and final salvation. There were both a simplicity of faith and that intense brotherly love which had their practical demonstration in the equal distribution of temporal possessions. The community of goods did not arise from a divine command, but was merely the natural effect of that broad charity which arose from the love of Christ and the possession of the Spirit. Its real majesty lay in its spontaneous quality. All thoughts centred in the memory of Christ as a personal Saviour, and in the consciousness of his continued presence. To crown all, there was a fervor in communicating the gospel which knew no bounds. The whole world seemed small. Its farthest horizon alone was to be the limit of teaching. What the apostles had felt and known was now their sole passion. There was little difference between the apostle and the unlettered believer. Each, in his own best way, was to preach the new life in Christ, that all men might share its sacrifice here and its holy joy hereafter. Pentecost was the practical divine testimony to the universal adoption of the gospel. The removal of the natural limitations of language was a divine indication of the application of Christianity to every class and condition. It was the divine endorsement of the command to the disciples to preach and teach the Word throughout the world.

Chapter II.

THE SCENE OF THE LABORS OF THE APOSTLES.

1. The Acts of the Apostles are the chief source of information concerning the fields of work of the different apostles. But the epistles of Paul and his associates contain frequent statements which serve to supply missing links in that more formal history. To these may be added the supplementary accounts of writers from the second century to the fourth; many of which, however, are only vague suppositions, or impressions, which existed in oral form in the early Church.

2. Peter represented the Jewish type of Christianity. He was slow to learn that Christianity was designed for all men. Pentecost should have been enough, but even this great lesson did not satisfy his intensely Jewish character. After important labors in Palestine, extending as far north as Antioch, he came to the council in Jerusalem, and united with Paul in removing all Jewish ceremonials as a condition of entrance into the Church. Here, at the moment of supreme test, he wisely changed his position. Henceforth all bonds with Judaism were broken, and Jews and Gentiles became Christians on precisely the same terms. There are good reasons to suppose that Peter made an evangelistic tour through portions of Asia Minor, for his first epistle intimates previous labors in Pontus, Galatia, Cappadocia, Asia (the province), and Bithynia. He also says that at the time of writing he was in Babylon. If this was the Babylon on the banks of the Euphrates, he was, no doubt, attracted thither by reason of the large Jewish population resident there. It seems to have been understood by him and Paul that he should confine his labors to the east, while Paul should occupy himself with the west.

3. Peter in Rome. There is no historical proof that Peter founded the Church in Rome, or that he was ever there. His residence there is not mentioned by the earliest writers in their lists of the first bishops of the western metropolis. The first mention was by Dionysius of Corinth, A.D. 170, who speaks of Peter's death in Rome. But while we are without definite proof of Peter's presence in Rome, it is not impossible that he did spend a brief period there, and that he died about the year 67, in the persecution under Nero.

4. Paul towers far above all the apostles in the majesty of his character, the scope of his genius, the depth of his learning, and the sublime quality of his labors. Educated in both Jewish and pagan learning, after his miraculous conversion he became an apostle, in every sense able to cope with the antagonism of the combined foes of his age. His call was to the Gentiles. He made three great missionary tours. The first was begun A.D. 44, and embraced Cyprus, and then Asia Minor, where he visited Perga, Pisidia, Antioch, Iconium, Lystra, and Derbe. His second began A.D. 48. He went northward through Syria into Asia Minor, and visited Cilicia, Phrygia, Galatia. He then crossed the Ægean Sea to Macedonia. He began his European ministry in Philippi, and went thence southward into Greece as far as Corinth. From thence he went to Ephesus, and returned to Jerusalem. He entered upon his third tour A.D. 52. He went again into Asia Minor, taking Galatia, Phrygia, and Troas on the way. He then crossed into Macedonia and Illyricum. He returned to Troas, and, passing by the Ægean islands, proceeded back to Jerusalem. Here he was arrested, and taken a prisoner to Cæsarea, where he was two years in confinement. He appealed for justice to Cæsar, and was taken to Rome. He remained there from A.D. 59 to 61. He was now released, and, as we believe, entered on a fourth tour, embracing a visit to Crete, Macedonia, Corinth, Nicopolis, Dalmatia, and Asia Minor. He was a second time arrested, and taken to Rome. He suffered martyrdom in Nero's reign, A.D. 66.

5. **John** represented the mediating element between Judaism and paganism. His attachment and scene of labor seem to have been, for the first twenty years after Pentecost, chiefly in Palestine. He was present at the council in Jerusalem, A.D. 50. For twenty years, or until A.D. 70, we lose sight of him entirely. The probability is, that he labored in the valley of the Tigris and Euphrates, with Babylon as the centre, and returned to Jerusalem, whence he fled to Ephesus on the capture of that city by Titus. We find him now in Ephesus. His residence was intermitted by his exile to the island of Patmos. He died in Ephesus about A.D. 98, when about one hundred years old.

6. **The Labors of the other Apostles** are largely matter of conjecture, derived from the writings of Hegesippus, Eusebius, and Nicephorus, who framed their suppositions from the floating oral traditions in the Christian communities. James the Elder suffered martyrdom in Jerusalem, about A.D. 44. James, our Lord's brother, preached in Jerusalem, and finally died there a martyr. It was believed that Philip labored in Phrygia; Simon

Zelotes, in Egypt and the neighboring African coast; Thomas, in India; Andrew, in Scythia, Asia Minor, Thrace, and Greece; Matthias, in Ethiopia; Judas, called Lebbæus or Thaddeus, in Persia; and Bartholomew, in Lycaonia, Armenia, and India.

7. **The uncertainty as to fields of labor** of most of the apostles is one of the marvels of the Scriptures. One fact is clear, however, that the trend of the world's Christian life was westward. On the distribution of the gospel into the more stable parts of the Roman Empire we have full light in the labors of Paul. All the just and vital interests of Christianity centred in that one man's work. Rome was to be the point of departure for the sowing of the truth in the north and farther west. Here Paul brought his life and labors to a triumphant close. But with his martyrdom he had only begun his work. His example and writings—and the two are inseparable—have been, ever since, the permanent and necessary treasures of the Church. The present current of the truth is a reversal of the old order. It is from the fields then barbarous, and largely unknown to the geography of those times, towards the old East. What the apostles could only begin will be completed, in the eastern countries, by the laborers sent out from the warm heart of western Protestantism.

Chapter III.

THE GREEK AND ROMAN CONDITIONS.

1. The Two Forces. The pagan literature, in the earliest period of Christianity, was a beautiful piece of human workmanship. No temple in stone was so symmetrical and elaborate as that of Greek and Roman letters. From rude beginnings, it had grown into such majestic and firm proportions that, to this day, it challenges the admiration of the world. The classic achievements in the whole field of literature, art, philosophy, and legislation are the common inheritance of man. When Christianity came forward with its strange claims upon the confidence of men, there was but little in its exterior which could awaken sympathy. The most despised land had produced it. Its founder had suffered death on the ignominious cross. Its first apostles were of humble origin, and, with the exception of Paul, not one had drunk at the classic fountains. That a new faith, with such multiform disadvantages, should venture upon such a hostile field, where the literature and traditions of many centuries held firm ground, seemed a hopeless task. But the heroism of the first preachers of Christianity was not disturbed by the number or strength of the enemy. The promise of success was the basis of their faith. They wrought on, and expected triumph over every foe. Which should win —the obscure Christian, who had never fought a battle, or the cultivated pagan, who had never lost one?

2. The Greeks. The path of the Greek to mastery had been through all fields of intellectual development. Out of the old Pelasgic cradle he had grown to the full grandeur of Attic manhood. The blood of many tribes flowed through his veins, and he had absorbed the strongest and best elements of all. In epic and dramatic poetry he produced Homer, Hesiod, Æschylus, Sophocles, and Euripides. The Greek was a lover of form and color. He caught his inspiration from the wild and beautiful scenery of his islands and broken coast. Apelles and Phidias became the incarnation of his passion. In his long battle for federation he had produced such great law-givers as Solon and Lycurgus. He was of fervent temperament, and, living always in a feverish political atmosphere, he had developed Demosthenes, Æschines, and Isocrates—orators who have swayed audiences in all later ages.

3. The Philosophical Systems. In philosophy, the Greeks labored with great industry. The growth of their systems was contemporaneous with their national prosperity. The dealing with the fundamental questions of human being and destiny by Socrates and Plato reveals a deep moral purpose. There are two great periods of Greek philosophy, separated by the downfall of Alexander's empire. The former extends from B.C. 600 to B.C. 324. Within this short space arose all the best thinkers, who founded the Ionic, the early Pythagorean, the Eleatic, the Atomistic, and the Sophist Schools. The culmination was reached in the three systems of Socrates, Plato, and Aristotle. The second period extends from B.C. 324 to A.D. 530. The schools of the decadence rose and fell at this time—the Stoics, the Epicureans, and the Sceptics. To this was added Neo-Platonism, founded by Plotinus. The most spiritual of the entire circle of Greek philosophers was Plato. In many departments of his philosophy, such as the unity and spirituality of God and the immortality of the soul, he made, though unconsciously, very near approaches to the truths of revelation. It was the habit of early Christian teachers to regard his system as kindred to Christianity. Eusebius said: "Plato alone, of all the Greeks, reached the vestibule of truth, and stood upon its threshold." Justin Martyr, Clemens of Alexandria, Origen, and Augustine, in the early period, and Schleiermacher and Neander in the recent period, were led to Christ through Plato as their guide.

4. The Decay of the Greek Philosophy. The best systems in the group declined with the political supremacy of the Greek confederation. Those which succeeded the loss of national independence were the systems of despair. When Christianity arose, the prevailing Greek philosophy was sceptical. The mythology had lost its firm hold, while philosophy, which was the substitute offered by the profoundest thinkers, proved its own inability to satisfy the cravings of the soul for salvation, and the solution of its great problems. Both pagan faith and thought were unavailing to meet the spiritual wants of man. The soul could not live on the triumphs of art, or literature, or eloquence, or legislation. Christianity came forward with its sublime truths, and made proffer of them to the world. Paul, preaching Christ on Mars Hill, looked back upon a long pathway of dead systems of Greek genius, and forward upon the rise of Christian creations in their place. Great as had been the thinkers of the Stoa and the Academy, greater still was the messenger of Christ. His system was the permanent truth.

5. The Roman Empire. When Christianity began its career for the world's possession, the Roman rule was universal. The literature and religion were shaped from Greek models. But the Romans gave to everything a practical direction. Law was their habit, and to govern was their passion. They had no sooner conquered a rude tribe than they converted the territory into a new province, and gave it all the qualities of a firm part of the empire. Palestine was an integral part of the great domain, governed by Roman deputies, who were closely watched at the same time that they were intrusted with large authority. Paul, the Greek preacher, enjoyed and asserted the rights of Roman citizenship. Great highways, built at great expense for the rapid movement of armies, connected all parts of the broad territory. These made easy the rapid dissemination of the gospel. The apostles could move along these stone roads with ease, and so convert paths for soldiers into highways for the triumphant march of the messengers of the peaceful gospel.

6. Obstacles. The difficulties confronting the Church throughout the Roman Empire were, however, of formidable character. The entire body of the people was hostile to any spiritual religion. What did not appeal to the senses had no attraction to them as an object of worship. The hold of the old mythology was lost, and a general scepticism as to all beliefs prevailed. But the emperors regarded the preservation of the ancestral faith as the great bulwark of the throne. Political government and fidelity to the prevailing mythology were held to be inseparable. Hence, Christianity was bitterly opposed, so soon as its antagonism was discovered. It was seen to be hostile to the elaborate temple service. The emperor, who was also Pontifex Maximus, or supreme priest, was held responsible for the support of the state religion. The temples and pagan rites must be sustained. The more closely Christianity came into view, the more stringent became the measures for its suppression. The Christians made no concealments. They absented themselves from the temples, threw off all faith in the ruling mythology, and openly declared their hostility to it.

7. Moral Destitution of Paganism. When Christianity appeared the moral depravity of the Roman Empire was at its lowest ebb. The stricter morals of the republic had disappeared in the wild licentiousness of the empire. It was an age of excesses, which the satirists, with Juvenal and Persius at their head, held up to universal contempt.

(*a*) The degradation of women was complete. Even in Athens the wife was a slave, and possessed no legal rights. She could bequeath only a measure of barley to her offspring. Her present depression in Turkey is a fair picture of the old pagan conditions. Her mental endowments were declared to be of inferior grade. She was supposed to excel in duplicity and treachery. Marriage was a loose bond, with only the shadow of political institution.

(*b*) A low estimate was placed on childhood. In Sparta the maimed children were a burden to the state, because useless as soldiers. Only boys had an importance in the eye of parents. Stealing was a virtue in a boy, provided he could do it so cleverly as not to be detected. Socrates, Plato, and Aristotle never went so far as to enforce the element of religion in education. Children were not taught reverence for their parents. Jupiter, the son of Saturn, hurled his father from the throne, shut him up in Tartarus, and parcelled out the universe between himself and his two brothers, Neptune and Pluto. With this picture of filial brutality as the basis of the pagan mythology, what better estimate could be expected of childhood? All the types of parental love were based on admiration of heroic deeds. When Xenophon was told that his son had died in battle, he replied: "I did not request the gods to make my son immortal or long-lived, for it is not clear that this was suitable for him; but that he might have integrity in his principles, and be a lover of his country, and now I have my desire." Children, according to the pagan thought, were only machines for fighting future battles. Christ achieved no greater revolution than when he elevated childhood into equality with manhood. His one declaration: "Of such is the kingdom of heaven," was a fatal blow at the world's prevailing estimate of children.

(*c*) Slavery was universal. It underlay the whole political and social structure. In Attica, as early as B.C. 309, according to Demetrius Phalereus, there were twenty thousand citizens and four hundred thousand slaves. Among the Romans the slaves were not regarded as persons (*personæ*), but as things (*res*). The doors of the wealthy Romans were guarded by *ostiarii*, or slaves, in chains, who lay like dogs before their kennels. When a gentleman was murdered, and his assassin could not be found, the crime was supposed to have been committed by a slave, and all the slaves, with their wives and children, were put to death, to make sure of the offender. Tacitus says that, when Pedanius Secundus was murdered, as many as four hundred innocent slaves were put to death. Slavery extended to all parts of the empire, and the number in Rome was constantly kept up by the inflow of captives in the wars.

CHAPTER IV.

THE ATTITUDE OF JUDAISM TOWARDS CHRISTIANITY.

1. The Jewish Antecedents. The Jews regarded themselves as the world's teachers and law-givers. They alone, of all peoples, believed in the unity of God. Their history was a long chapter of splendor and defeat. When they escaped from Egyptian bondage, and reached Palestine, their first form of government was republican, or the rule of the Judges. From this they degenerated into a monarchy, which, after the death of Solomon, was divided into two kingdoms—Israel and Judah. Unity in both government and faith was gone. Israel was overcome by the Assyrians, and Judah by the Babylonians, and both nations were led off into exile to the valley of the Tigris and the Euphrates. Only a small portion of Israel, or the ten tribes, returned. The captives of conquered Judah were cured of their polytheistic tendencies, and, preserving their identity under Cyrus and his Persian successors, returned to Palestine. After the dissolution of the empire of Alexander the Great, who had conquered Palestine B.C. 323, the Seleucidæ ruled in Syria and the Ptolemies in Egypt. Between these two the Jews led a subject and timid life, and finally submitted to the Seleucidæ. The Greek religion was foisted upon them. But they rebelled, and determined to preserve their old faith, and to conquer their rulers. Mattathias and his three sons led the revolt. For a time they were successful, and hoped to restore the old Davidic splendor. Pompey was at this time in Asia, at the head of the Roman army. He was invited to settle the dispute. He entered the country, besieged Jerusalem B.C. 63, and, as was the Roman wont, took possession of the country, and united it with the Roman Empire. The Jews had now lost all independence. Their later revolts had no other effect than to tighten the Roman hold, and to disperse small bodies of colonists around the eastern coasts of the Mediterranean.

2. The Samaritans were a mongrel religious body. They consisted of returned Jews from Assyria, who brought with them those elements of pagan worship which they had absorbed during their captivity. They settled in the valley of Shechem, and built their temple on the top of Mount Gerizim. The sect still exists, and consists of about one hundred and fifty people. Their city is Nablus, which lies in the valley between Mounts Gerizim and Ebal. They have a high-priest, and are still in possession of their revered copy of the Pentateuch, believed to be the oldest in the world.

3. Other Jewish Bodies. The Pharisees were the most educated of all Jewish classes. Their teachers were versed in the law, and represented the hopes, the narrowness, and the ritualism of the people. They taught a national revival. They originated as a class about B.C. 144, and aimed to restore the waning faith to its old Mosaic strength. Inclined to allegorical interpretation, and devoted to traditions, they aimed to supplement the Scriptures by traditional accretions. The Sadducees originated with Zadoc, who lived about B.C. 250. They strove to restore Mosaism, but rejected tradition. They absorbed some of the elements of pagan thought, especially the doctrines of Epicurus.

They rejected angels, the resurrection of the body, the immortality of the soul, and the divine interference in human affairs. The Essenes originated about B.C. 150. Their belief was as much Persian as Jewish. They held the sun to be a living being, and that virtue and vice inhered in matter. They led a monastic life, and practised community of goods. All of these sects were in full strength at the time of Christ. The Essenes were retired, but the Pharisees and Sadducees were strong and prominent. But all the sects disappeared with the destruction of Jerusalem by Titus, A.D. 70.

4. The Jews of the Dispersion. The Jews are the wanderers of all history and all continents. From the time of their captivity in Assyria and Babylonia down to the present day, they have held their pilgrim staff in hand. About B.C. 350 we find a large colony on the shore of the Caspian Sea. Syria, under the reign of Seleucus Nicator (B.C. 312–328), received a vast Jewish population. In the insecure interval between Alexander the Great and A.D. 70, they had gone, in colonies, into Assyria, Mesopotamia, Armenia, Asia Minor, Crete, Cyprus, and the Ægean Islands. In Lydia and Phrygia there was a colony of two thousand families. They generally preserved their identity.

5. The Jews of Alexandria. The most concentrated Jewish population outside of Palestine was in northern Africa. Egypt, Lybia, and Cyrene abounded in Jews. Alexandria was their chief centre. Even under Alexander, the founder of the city, large numbers settled there, while he assigned eight thousand Samaritans to the Thebaid. Extensive privileges were granted the Jews. They not only thrived in commerce, but developed thorough and broad scholarship. Philo, who attempted to harmonize Jewish theology and Greek philosophy, was a Jew, whose learning was profound, and worthy of high praise. The Greek version of the Old Testament, the Septuagint, was a great triumph of Jewish learning.

6. The Roman Jews. The first Jewish colony in Rome consisted of captives brought by Pompey from Palestine. They were assigned a distinct part of the city, which they have occupied ever since—the present Ghetto. Julius Cæsar granted the Jews special favors. They were declared freedmen (*libertini*), had their synagogues, observed their festivals, and held the Sabbath as a sacred day. The cultivated Romans, however, always despised them. They were the usual objects of raillery and satire. Juvenal held them up to contempt by saying that they prayed to nothing but the clouds and the empty heavens.

7. The Jewish Colonies as Apostolic Fields. The apostles observed a common plan in preaching the gospel. They went first to the Jews, and then appealed to the outlying populations. Paul's success among them was often signal, but from them came also his most bitter foes. There were great advantages in making the Jews his first auditors. They were already familiar with the sacred history antecedent to Christianity. They had heard of the marvellous career of Jesus. Their annual visits to Jerusalem, to attend the festivals, had made them acquainted with the popular estimate of the new gospel. "To the Jew first," was his invariable plan. But there was no long pause. "Also to the Greek," was the next step of the tireless preacher.

Chapter V.

THE PERIOD OF UNIVERSAL PERSECUTION.

1. The Jewish Hostility. The political prostration of the Jews embittered them against the Christians. There was nothing in common between the Jewish sects and the early Church. The scepticism of the Sadducees and the disappointed hopes of the Pharisees combined to intensify the popular hate. The council in Jerusalem cast Peter and John into prison, and put Stephen to death. A general persecution, under Herod Agrippa, A.D. 44, broke out, and James the Elder fell a victim to its rage. The Christians took refuge in Pella, beyond the Jordan. Bar-cochba led a final popular Jewish revolt against the Roman authority, A.D. 132, but was defeated by Julius Severus, and Jerusalem became a heap of ruins. The Roman emperor Hadrian tried to destroy the attachment of the Christians to the sacred associations of the city by erecting on Calvary a temple to Venus, and, over the Holy Sepulchre, a statue to Jupiter. But his efforts, while pleasing to the Jews, had no material effect. The Jews, now that all hope of national independence was gone, established a school at Tiberias, where they tried to achieve with the pen what they had failed to accomplish by the sword. Their misrepresentations of Christ and his doctrines formed an important element in the general literary attack on Christianity during the first three centuries.

2. The Outbreak of the Pagan Persecution. Christianity soon extended beyond Jewish bounds, and became a thing which might well arouse the fears of the whole Roman Empire. In Rome the Christians were regarded as simply a new Jewish sect. And when, in the middle of the first century, a disturbance arose among the Jews of Rome, both Jews and Christians were banished by the emperor Claudius. Nero represented the popular hostility to Christianity. He was believed to have set fire to Rome, where the flames had full sway for nine days. He threw the blame, however, on the Christians, and resorted to the most barbarous methods to show his rage. He even had some Christians smeared with pitch and burned alive, while he caused others to be sewn in the skins of wild beasts and thrown out to the dogs. The persecution continued until his death. Under Domitian (A.D. 81–96) a milder policy of hostility was observed, the oppression of the Christians being chiefly confined to exile and the seizure of their property.

3. The Grounds of Hostility. The twelve tables of the Roman law forbade the existence of foreign faiths within the dominions, but the habit had been to conciliate the conquered provinces by toleration of the existing religions. The appearance of the Christians, however, was the signal for revival of the old prohibition. The bonds uniting the Christians were close. Their separate services were declared an act of hostility to the country. They were accused of disobedience to the laws, and of a spirit ripe at any moment for insurrection. They were charged with immoral practices in their services. All popular calamities, such as earthquakes, inundations, pestilence, and defeat in war, were attributed to them. A popular proverb ran thus: "Deus non pluit—duc ad Christianos!" "It does not rain—lead us against the Christians!" Tertullian has left this record of the Roman habit of charging the disciples of Christ with all possible calamities: "If the Tiber overflow its banks, if the Nile does not water the fields, if the clouds refuse rain, if the earth shake, if famine or storms prevail, the cry always is, 'Pitch the Christians to the lions!'"

4. New Persecutions. Trajan (A.D. 98–117) continued the policy of his predecessors, but in milder form. He gave orders to the proconsul Pliny, in Bithynia, not to seek out the Christians, but, when charges were brought against them, to give them opportunity to recant, and, in case of refusal, to sacrifice them to the gods. The persecution under Trajan extended to Palestine and Syria. Under Hadrian (A.D. 117–138) and Antoninus Pius (A.D. 138–161) the popular fury against the Christians increased to great violence. While these emperors granted the Church no favor, their attitude was less hostile than that of some of their predecessors. Marcus Aurelius (A.D. 161–180) was thoughtful and calm. He was a Stoic by profession, and, while he had no warm reverence for the national religion, he showed no sympathy with the Christians. He was repelled by their devotion to Christ and their readiness to suffer. He tolerated violence, and under him the persecutions at Smyrna, where Polycarp suffered martyrdom, and at Lyons and Vienne, in Gaul, took place.

5. Alternate Rest and Persecution. There was now a slight relaxation of violence, but under Septimius Severus (A.D. 193–211) the Christians were treated with cruelty. The persecution was widespread, and the martyrdoms were numerous. Alexander Severus professed to be an Eclectic in faith, and regarded Jesus as one of the gods. He placed a bust of Christ beside those of Abraham, Orpheus, and Apollonius of Tyana. He instituted no active measures of hostility. Decius had but a short reign (A.D. 249–251), and yet he improved his time industriously by endeavoring to exterminate the Christians. His persecution was general, and as violent as that under Nero.

6. Final Efforts to Destroy Christianity. The reign of Decius was succeeded by a brief interval of peace, which was brought to a close by the hostile attitude of Valerian (A.D. 253–260). Under Aurelian, Diocletian, Galerius, and Maximinus the persecution raged with varied fury. Great political complications arose. The changes in the imperial succession were frequent, and new methods of repression of the Christians were constantly adopted. During the whole time, however, the Christian Church grew in numbers and aggressive force. From A.D. 64 to 313, when Constantine granted an edict of toleration to the Christians, persecutions prevailed about seventy years. All forms of torture and violent death were adopted. There was no security at home. The exiles were numerous, but the Christians carried their faith and life with them to their new places of abode, where they built up societies, which in turn became centres for the wider dissemination of the gospel. Christianity had conquered in the realm of political life. It was now safe from the hand of any Roman ruler.

CHAPTER VI.

CHRISTIAN WORSHIP.

1. Simplicity of Forms. The Christians were at first greatly attached to the temple in Jerusalem. They met within its precincts. There was no disposition to erect separate sanctuaries, and, had there been, the means to meet the expense were too limited. In time, however, the hostility of the Jews made it impossible to convene in either the temple or any room near it. The Christians were, therefore, driven to private houses, where one room served the purpose of a sanctuary. A small platform (*cathedra*) served for the speaker or reader, while a table (*ara*) was used for the celebration of the Lord's Supper.

2. Order of Service. The services consisted chiefly of reading selections from the Old Testament, the apostolical epistles, and, latest of all, the gospels. The reading was attended with copious exposition. The day of the elaborate homily, with a short scriptural passage as a mere motto, had not yet arrived. All that was said was meant to give to the hearer a deeper knowledge of the divine word. Singing of psalms and hymns was an important part of the service. It might be led by an individual, but the music was by the whole congregation. The Psalms of David and the rhythmic parts of the prophecies furnished the favorite basis. Prayer was connected with the singing, and the congregation responded "Amen" at the close. The concluding part of the service was the Lord's Supper. Until about A.D. 150, the agape, or love-feast, was connected with the communion service, but, because of its abuse, was afterwards separated from it. After the prayer the kiss of charity was given, and the apostolical benediction was pronounced.

3. **The Sacraments.** There were two sacraments in the early church — the Lord's Supper and Baptism. After the council at Jerusalem, which abrogated the Jewish initiatory ceremonial as necessary for admission to the Church, baptism was held to be the only visible condition of reception. The formula, "In the name of the Father, Son, and Holy Ghost," was observed from the beginning of the Apostolic Church.

4. **The Sabbath,** or seventh day, continued to be observed by the Christians who had entered the Church from Judaism. But the Sunday, or first day of the week, was also observed, in memory of our Lord's resurrection. Gradually the Sunday became more prominent, and, finally, the observance of the seventh day was discontinued entirely. Those members of the Church who had been Jews were inclined to regard with reverence the festivals to which they had been accustomed in their former communion. These, however, they relinquished, with the exception of two, Easter and Pentecost, to which also the Gentile Christians adhered, as these festivals commemorated two great events in Christian history—our Lord's resurrection and the descent of the Spirit.

Chapter VII.

THE LIFE OF CHRISTIANS.

1. Contrast with Paganism. Every part of Christian life was in direct antagonism to that of the pagan Greeks and Romans. The Christians obliterated all social and national differences. No sooner was a new member received than he found himself in the midst of a brotherhood. "These Christians," says Bunsen, "belonged to no nation and to no state; but their fatherland in heaven was to them a reality, and the love of the brethren, in truth and not in words, made the Christian congregation the foreshadowing of a Christian commonwealth, and a model for all ages to come."

2. Care of the Needy. The relief of the poor and suffering received early attention. Paul collected contributions from the Greek Christians in Asia Minor for the poor in Jerusalem. All his epistles prove that the poor in each society were constantly in his mind. No needy body of believers was forgotten in its silent sorrow. When, later, persecutions became violent and widespread, the spirit of apostolic sympathy was sustained in all its fervor. The pagans neglected their needy. Their religion had no heart. But the Christians sought out the suffering, and helped them with lavish hand. During the pestilence in North Africa, in the middle of the third century, the pagans deserted their sick and dying, and stripped their bodies of valuables, while the Christians divided their means with the suffering, cleared the streets of decomposing bodies, and nursed the sick with tenderness and devotion.

3. Elevation of Woman. The early prominence given to woman was an important factor. Elizabeth, Anna, and Mary the mother of Jesus became early witnesses, however unconscious, to the dignity and worth of woman in the Christian system. The women mentioned by Paul in his epistles were examples of devotion and wisdom in the spread of the gospel. In times of persecution woman presented a sublime spectacle of readiness and composure in the hour of death. Perpetua and Felicitas, who cheerfully welcomed martyrdom, became types of womanly heroism in every part of Christendom.

4. The Slave. Christianity applied its humane spirit to the slave. Paul's chart of freedom ran thus: "There is neither bond nor free." The slave, the moment he became a Christian, became a brother with his master. As Christianity expanded, its tendency was to bring the oppressed and the oppressor together, upon a common plane of brotherly equality. Paul's appeal to Philemon, to show kindness to the slave Onesimus, and receive him back again, was an index of the power of Christianity to soften, and even obliterate, all the asperity attendant upon bondage in man.

5. The Social Revolution. Christianity triumphed not only in the broad field of territorial expansion, but in the more subtile department of the whole structure of social life. Paganism was only a whited sepulchre. Its splendor was an exterior thing alone. It created no happy homes, for woman was without worth, and children were no blessing. Wherever the Christians lived they built up happy households.

Chapter VIII.

ECCLESIASTICAL ORGANIZATION.

1. The Divine and Human Elements. The constitution of the early Church was in part of divine ordering. But this was only in outline. The apostolate was fundamental and original, but temporary. It was designed as the great introductory force, which should cease so soon as it had served its purpose. From this, as a basis, the permanent orders of presbyter and deacon developed. A large measure of liberty was left to the judgment of the Church, as new exigencies and larger growth might demand.

2. The Temporary Officers. To these belonged the apostles. The condition was, that the apostle must have seen Christ, in the flesh or in his risen state. Their work was evangelistic and organizing. Then came the prophets. They were inspired by the Holy Ghost for the special work of teaching higher revelations. Foretelling events was not their controlling function, but the revelation of God's will, especially in the choice of persons for great service in the Church. The prophet was not necessarily an apostle, but the apostle was a prophet. Paul, Agabus, Simeon, Barnabas, Manaen, Judas the Evangelist, and Silas belonged to the prophetic class. To them came the evangelists. They were preachers without defined limits, and were aids to the apostles, or, as Rothe says, "apostolic delegates." Their work was preparatory,—the preaching in new societies until organization was established. Philip, Timothy, Titus, Silas or Silvanus, Luke, John, Mark, Clement, and Epaphras belonged to the evangelist class.

3. The Permanent Officers. (*a*) *Bishops and Elders.* Here were, first of all, the bishops or presbyters. The word bishop (*episcopos*) was of Greek origin, and was in common use among both Greeks and Romans as a political supervisor. The societies of the West, which consisted of members from paganism, used the word for the chief or superintending pastor, as they were already familiar with it. The converts from Judaism naturally took the synagogue as their model, and as the elder pastor (*presbuteros*) was the chief or superintending pastor of the synagogue, they applied it to the chief pastor of the Christian Church. There was not the least difference in the original duties of the bishop and the presbyter. In each case he was the spiritual head of one church or society. Later, when churches increased, and the supervising office was of wider scope, the Western word supplanted the Eastern, and the term bishop was used, while that of presbyter went into the background. But the bishop, in the early and pure period of the Church, was of no higher order than the presbyter. The duties of one were those of both: "To feed the flock of God . . . taking the oversight thereof" (1 Peter v. 2).

(*b*) *Deacons.* These were both an order and an office. The duties are minutely described in the Scriptures (Acts vi. 1–8). They aided the apostles, had care of the poor and sick, assisted in administering the Lord's Supper, and preached. The deaconesses were a special office, designed for caring for the sick, the aged, the female poor, and the instruction of orphans.

Chapter IX.

EBIONISM AND GNOSTICISM.

1. Disposition to make Terms. Christianity was making steady progress in every field. Some of the more advanced thinkers in both Judaism and paganism saw in the Christian system so much that commended itself to universal confidence that each proposed to adapt it to his own faith and philosophy. This was a new plan, more dangerous to Christianity by far than outward opposition. In each case the overture was strengthened by people within the Christian fold, who responded to the flattering proposition, though without representing the spirit of the whole body.

2. The Ebionites. After the council in Jerusalem which settled the great Pauline principle of the freedom of Christian converts from the Mosaic law, there remained a body of Christians who would not accept the conclusion. Jerusalem was their centre. They were of two classes—those who saw in Christianity the fulfilment of all that was worthy in Judaism, and those who were more conservative, and refused to acknowledge the new faith as the culmination of Mosaism. Out of these two tendencies sprang Ebionism. They held that the Mosaic law was still in force ; its close observance was a necessity for salvation; Christianity fulfilled the law, but did not abrogate it; Christ was the prophet of Israel's deliverance; he was a mere man; his generation was natural; the Divine Spirit entered him at baptism; Christ was a good Jew; his piety was his claim to Messiahship; he performed miracles; and he supplemented the law by his own commands. The Ebionites rejected Paul's writings, as not Jewish enough. They had communities in Asia Minor, Cyprus, and in Rome, and existed down to the fourth century.

3. The Nazaræans more nearly approached Christianity. They accepted Paul's writings, and held that Christ was the Son of God, and that his generation was divine. They disappeared in the fourth century. The Elcesaites, or Sampsæans, were of similar Jewish proclivities, but had a stronger Oriental element in their faith. They kept the Jewish Sabbath, retained sacrifices, held that oil and salt are emblems of spiritual communication, and prayed with their faces towards the sun.

4. Gnosticism in General. This system was a combination of the new Platonic philosophy with Oriental theosophy, the two proposing to appropriate certain Christian elements. Philo, a learned Jew of Alexandria, born about A.D. 40, furnished the most decided contribution. He aimed to unite Judaism and Platonism. He regarded God and the world as forming a dualism, both finite and infinite. He believed that God could not assume visible form, but can reveal himself to the soul. The Logos is a divine emanation, which the Holy Spirit, the Divine Wisdom, imparted directly to the first men, and to all who have since striven after likeness to God. From the fundamental ideas of Philo the great Gnostic system developed into special systems, but all of them were strained accommodations to Christian ideas.

5. Jewish Gnosticism. Cerinthus (A.D. 100) was the

earliest representative. He held that Judaism was the world's preparation for Christianity; that Jesus was the natural son of Joseph and Mary, and arrived at his pure state at baptism and by his holy life; that his death was not a mediatorial service; but that he would come again, and establish a vast earthly kingdom. Basilides taught in Alexandria about A.D. 130. He held that the universe is a dualism—deity and matter. Between these there is a great multitude of æons, or emanations from God, who record his glory and make it fruitful. Each nation is ruled by an æon. The Jewish æon taught by means of Moses and the prophets. But truth was universal—Greek, Jews, and Persians shared it. The highest æon was recorded to Jesus at his baptism. Basilides was cautious, not committing himself to any of the extremes which constituted the body of the Gnostic system. Valentinian (A.D. 138) first taught in Alexandria, but afterwards removed to Rome. He was at first a Christian, but withdrew from the Church. He borrowed his chief ideas from Plato. His fundamental doctrine was emanation. The supreme God lives in silence and solitude. But, to be perfect, he must love, and in order to love there must be an object. So he began to emanate. The æons are personalities, which emanate from him. Man, the Logos, and the Church, are divine emanations. Man is redeemed through the Logos. The crucifixion represented the divine might by which the world is purified from sin. Valentinian was the founder of the largest Gnostic school. His chief disciples were Heracleon, Ptolemæus, and Bardesanes.

6. Oriental and Pagan Gnostics. The Ophites (serpent worshippers) were the first of this class. They existed as a small sect in Egypt at the time of Christ, and afterwards adopted a perverted type of Christianity, but retained a large measure of Oriental theosophy. The pleroma, or highest spirit, develops itself in æons; and from the fourth one there floats a ray of light, which combines with matter, and becomes the world-soul. Man is created. To defeat his elevation the serpent is prepared. The serpent becomes the type of all wisdom, and is worthy of worship. Man, by his fall, first arrives at the consciousness of freedom and mastery. There were two minor Ophite sects—the Cainites and the Sethians. Carpocrates built his system out of fragments of Buddhism and Neo-Platonism. He placed all faiths on the same plane—Orpheus, Pythagoras, Plato, and Christ were quite the same, according to him. His sect degenerated into wild libertinism. In Mani and the Manichæans we reach the limits of Oriental Gnosticism. Mani made the faith of Zoroaster the basis of his system, but added a superstructure of Buddhism and Christianity. Fatalism pervaded the whole structure. The sect continued down to the end of the third century, when Diocletian issued an edict for its suppression. The Ophites elevated man to supreme importance. Their estimate has been characterized in the following lines :

> "O thou citizen of Heaven!
> Thou much-praised Man!
> From thee comes Father,
> Through thee comes Mother,—
> Those two immortal names,
> The parents of the Æons."

7. Independent Gnosticism. Saturninus, who died about A.D. 174, held that the supreme Father has produced, by intermediate archangels and powers, seven angels, who are the sovereigns of the material world. Among them is the God of the Jews. Man was created, but with infirmities. The Saviour came to aid him towards final development. Tatian was a native of Assyria, but emigrated to Rome. His chief tenet was antagonism to marriage. He died about A.D. 174. The Encratites and Hudropastrians were followers of Tatian. The tendency to decline was manifested in all the Gnostic schools. Marcion and his followers represented the reformatory movement. He lived about A.D. 150. He avoided all the extremes of his predecessors, but leaned towards Christianity. He recognized Paul as the only veritable apostle, admitted one gospel, a distortion of Luke, and rejected all tradition and esoteric doctrines. In his later years he is said to have regretted his Gnostic vagaries, and to have sought readmission to the Church. Of all Gnostics he was the nearest approach to the true Christian.

8. The Place of Gnosticism. The service which Gnosticism rendered to the Church was to make the pagan mind acquainted with some fundamental Christian truths, to disintegrate the fabric of the pagan philosophy, and to prove, by its own fruitless endeavors, the impossibility of combining any system with Christianity. The Gnostics were a proud class. They set out with claims to all knowledge, approached Christianity as they would any other faith, and proposed to weigh it in their own small balance. They made reason the test of religion, and were devoid of all appreciation of the spiritual life. The danger to Christianity of all the Gnostic systems was in winning Christians to the adoption of them. But the Christian teachers were prompt in giving warning of their corrupt nature, and no great secession to them ever occurred. The Christians, as a body, regarded the Gnostics with aversion, because of the claim of many of them that they believed in the best part of Christianity. While Marcion was the nearest approach to the Christian, the interview of Polycarp with him one day, as the two met in a street in Rome, indicates the Christian hostility to all Gnostics. Polycarp was stopped by Marcion, who said: "Do you not recognize me?" The father replied promptly: "Certainly I do. I know the first-born of Satan!"

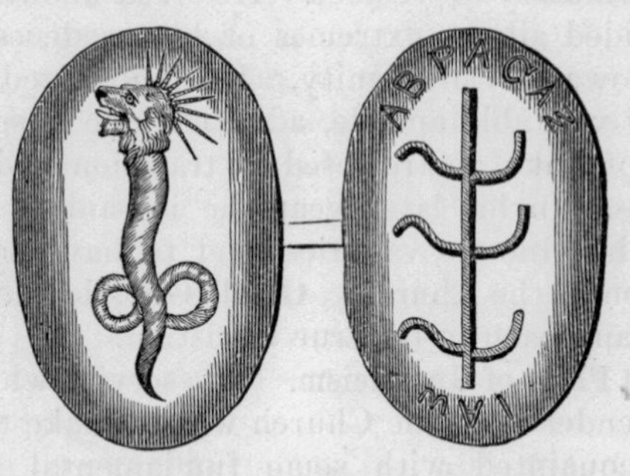

GNOSTIC SYMBOLS.

Chapter X.

THE PAGAN LITERARY ATTACK.

1. The Growing Importance of Christianity, in the mind of the pagan world, became very apparent in the attempts now made in literature to destroy its very foundations. By the beginning of the second century it became evident to the cultivated Romans that something more than imperial opposition was necessary to arrest the new faith. Every persecution left Christianity more solid, aggressive, and hopeful than it found it. During the second and third centuries the two hostile forces proceeded together—the sword and the pen. Each pursued its own path, and each hoped to win by help from the other. The Christians met the imperial opposition by non-resistance, but ceaseless evangelization. They met the antagonism of literature by such bold and masterful logic, and by such strong appeal to facts, that the whole structure of paganism was shaken by their arguments.

2. The Grounds for Pagan Alarm. The Greek and Roman writers saw in Christianity certain peculiarities well calculated to give them alarm. They had to deal with a new historical phenomenon. They saw, first, that the new religion was based upon certain writings, reaching back to the dawn of history, and culminating later in the life of the Founder and in the exposition of his doctrines; second, that there was an historical basis for Christianity; third, that it dealt with fundamental moral themes; fourth, that the people professing faith in the doctrines never grew weary of them; fifth, that the doctrines developed pure and heroic lives; sixth, that the scriptural cosmogony was more reasonable and consistent than that of Hesiod; seventh, that the character of Christ was without a blemish; and eighth, that his death had imparted to his followers a zeal which nothing had been able to arrest. To overcome such a system was a serious problem. But both Greek and Roman writers, with much self-consciousness, did not hesitate to undertake the task of demolition. The wise methods by which their work was met by Christian writers, and the fearless spirit in which the latter wrought, was a great surprise. It is one of the wonders of all literature.

3. General References. The hostile attitude of even general historians can be seen in mere allusions. Tacitus dismisses the subject by saying that Christ was the founder of a new sect, that he had been crucified by Pontius Pilate, that his system was a deadly superstition, and that the Christians were obnoxious to the human race. Antoninus says that the soul must be ready to leave the body by a mere obstinacy. Juvenal sneered at the Christian adoration of the heavens. Arrian reports Epictetus as protesting against the Galilean fearlessness of danger, and the doctrine that God created all things. Lucian was as severe on Christianity as on the other religions, all of which he cast into a common vortex of worthlessness. He called Christ a magician, and parodied the career of Jonah, our Lord's walking on the Sea of Galilee, and John's description of the New Jerusalem.

4. Celsus, Porphyry, and Hierocles were the strongest assailants of Christianity. Celsus lived about A.D. 150.

He held to a chief deity, a superintending providence, and the immortality of the soul. These views he derived from the Platonic philosophy. But when he examined Christianity, he lost sight of the parallel of these fundamental truths with the Christian system. His antagonism was bitter. He assailed the Old Testament, but levelled his attacks chiefly against the alleged weaknesses in the career and character of Jesus. Porphyry, born about A.D. 233, aimed to show that the pagan world presented higher magical characters than Jesus, and that the gospel history abounds in hopeless contradictions. His Candid Treatise against the Christians was an attempt to show a parallel between the sorcery of Apollonius of Tyana and Jesus, with a large balance in favor of the former.

5. General Charges against Christianity. Obscurer writers followed willingly in the footprints of the leaders. Satire, fiction, poetry, indeed all forms of literary effort, were employed to hold up Christianity to contempt. The principal grounds of hostility were:

1. The alleged contradictions in the Scriptures.

2. The uselessness of Christians to the existing state of society.

3. The philosophical absurdity of the Christian system.

4. The claim of the humanity of Jesus at the same time with that of divinity.

5. The immorality of Christians. This charge was based upon the secret meetings of Christians. It was never seriously believed. On the contrary, the moral life of believers stood out in beautiful contrast to the pagan immorality. That secrecy should be confounded with bad morals was natural to the pagan mind, familiar with the nameless licentiousness and wild commu-

nism connected with the Eleusinian and other mysteries. This and all the other charges were summed up by Tertullian in a single sentence, which he placed in the mouth of universal paganism, as its final argument against the Christians: "You have no right to exist!"

6. The Outcome of the Attack. The most which the pagan writers could hope from their attack was to prevent new accessions to the Church. They wrote for the pagan mind, not with any view to disturbing the Christian's faith in his own religion. This they were not so foolish as to imagine possible. The Christian body was too firmly knit to give ground for such a delusive expectation. No serious defection ever occurred because of the pagan attack. On the contrary, the numbers steadily increased. But the main object also failed completely. Paganism was in process of disintegration, and while the assailants flattered themselves that they were achieving a literary success, the result was a total disappointment. The pagan walls were falling too rapidly to be propped up. It was an effort for the impossible.

Chapter XI.

THE CHRISTIAN DEFENDERS.

1. The Two Classes. We now come to a brighter picture. The writing in defence of Christianity is called the *apology*, and the writer, an *apologist*. It is from the Greek word *apologia*, which meant a work written for resistance. But the apologies of the early Church were more than this. They were not only counter-arguments, but aggressive weapons. It was a fierce warfare upon the enemy's camp, followed by a hot pursuit. There were two classes of apologists, the Greek and the Latin, according to the territory which they occupied, and the language in which they wrote. But there were further differences. The Greeks belonged mostly to the second century, and their writings exhibited a profound intimacy with the Greek philosophy. Some of them had studied in the Greek schools, and entered the Church only in mature life. They endeavored to prove that Christianity was the blossom of all that was valuable in every system. They stood largely on the defensive. The Latins, on the other hand, were aggressive. They lived mostly in the third century, were more argumentative, wrote in a clearer and more methodical style, and carried the warfare into the hostile ranks with an energy equal to the Roman soldier on foreign battle-fields. Their perspective of Christianity was that of universal conquest and permanent dominion.

2. The Greeks. The principal Greek apologists were Aristo, Quadratus, Aristides, Justin, Melito, Miltiades, Irenæus, Athenagoras, Tatian, Clement of Alexandria, Hippolytus, and Origen. Aristo's dialogue between Papiskos and Jason was an attempt to prove the truth of Christianity and the messiahship of Jesus as the fulfilment of the Old Testament. Quadratus addressed an apology to Hadrian (A.D. 131), with a view to stop the persecution of the Christians. Aristides proved Christianity the culmination of the best systems in the classic world, and the one which should supersede all else. Justin wrote two apologies (A.D. 136 and A.D. 162), showing that the Christians were not responsible for public calamities; that they were true Roman citizens; that pagan philosophy and mythology abound in falsehood and contradiction; and that the only source of truth is the Scriptures. Athenagoras, in his Embassy of the Christians, applied a philosophical method to Christian defence. Tatian, who died about A.D. 176, wrote an Address to the Greeks, showing the ridiculous origin of the Greek religion and science. Clement, in his Pedagogue, and the Stromata, exposed the emptiness of the whole pagan fabric. Hippolytus wrote against the pagans, the Platonic philosophy, and the Jews. Origen, born A.D. 185, wrote eight books against Celsus, in which he exposed the weakness of the whole pagan structure.

3. The Latins. Tertullian stands at the head. His Apologeticus, written about A.D. 200, is the most brilliant piece of apologetic writing in the early Church. He showed that persecution was no final damage to the Christians. His other writings covered nearly every contested point. The supernatural element in Christianity was brought by him into great prominence, and defended with masterly skill. Cyprian wrote about the middle of the third century. His attack on pagan idolatry was merciless, and could not be answered. Arnobius (A.D. 297) surpassed all the apologists in his use of the miracles of Jesus, as a weapon of Christian attack. Lactantius, the Christian Cicero, wrote his Divine Institutions A.D. 320. His strength lay less in the force of his argument than in the purity and beauty of his style.

4. The Line of Defence. The objection that Christians were disloyal to the state was met by the answer that they were true to the emperor; obeyed all laws which did not interfere with Christianity; never conspired against the government; and never produced robbers, assassins, or traitors. Purity of life was proven as the outgrowth of pure doctrines. Tertullian said: "We live a life free from reproach. We live among you. You can see us every day." To the charge that national calamities were produced by the Christians, he replied: "Why do you suffer too? Why do your gods let you have these trials?" The inspiration of the Scriptures and purity of doctrine were fundamental arguments in all the apologetic writings. To these came the divine character of Jesus. When the assailants repelled the miraculous power of Jesus, the apologists replied: "Do you not say that your Æsculapius restores the lame and the halt; that your Orpheus, Zeno, and Kleanthes knew the Logos; and that Plato, in a letter to Hermeas and Koriskus, speaks of a son of God?" The purity of Christian morals was held up by the apologists in striking antagonism to the sensuality of paganism, which could produce only caricatures of good morals. The origin of the pagan gods was exposed with fearless skill. The apologists said, with Tatian, "What has become of your Juno, that she produces no more gods?" Arnobius said, defiantly: "Your gods abound in passion; some are drunkards, others are murderers, and multitudes are licentious."

5. The Triumph of the Apologists. When this battle of three centuries was over it was easy to see that the victory of the Christian writers was complete. It began with the pagan expectation of destroying the logical basis of Christianity, but ended by the exposure of the corruption of the Greek and Roman faith and the weakness of the boasted philosophy. Every department of Christian truth was defended by the apologists. Their arguments broke down the opposition, while they constitute a storehouse of Christian defence to which all later Christian writers have appealed with success. The indirect service of the attacks to the Church was great, in that all Christians were compelled to study the groundwork of Christianity, on every side. The laity were driven to read their Bible. The private member, over all Christendom, could give a reason for the faith that was in him. By the end of the fifth century the conflict was over. The apologists were the last to leave the field. The Christian now lived in a larger place. He was marching on to universal conquest. The words of one of the apologists expressed the attitude of all believers: "Every country is the Christian's fatherland, and every fatherland is the Christian's country."

Chapter XII.

THE CHRISTIAN SCHOOLS.

1. Early Attention to Christian Culture. From whatever side the Christian convert came he brought with him the love of the school. For ministerial training the Jews had, from distant times, the prophetic schools, under the care of their wisest teachers. In Athens, Tarsus, and Alexandria the Greeks possessed celebrated universities, which even Roman students attended, for the completion of studies pursued in Italy. The proper dealing with both Jewish and pagan thought made a thorough ministerial culture necessary. The preacher of the early Church lived in an atmosphere of opposition, and, to succeed, he must be well acquainted with not only the truth he would defend, but with the false system he would combat.

2. The Elements in Paul's Day. The whole tendency of Paul's character, career, and acquisitions was on the side of careful training. Timothy and Titus represented a group of young men who were inducted into Christianity through the labors of that apostle, and, by personal attendance on his journeys, were prepared to succeed him and the other apostles. It was a beautiful legend of the whole period that the aged John stood at the head of a theological school in Ephesus, whither young men flocked from all quarters to gather from him *memorabilia* of our Lord's ministry and personality.

3. The Alexandrian School. By the middle of the

second century there were three great Christian schools. The most important was that of Alexandria. This city was the chief seat of philosophical culture in the world after the destruction of the literary prestige of Athens. All currents of thought, from both East and West, flowed thither for two centuries. Plato, because of the sway of Neo-Platonism, was a familiar name. Here Christianity and pagan learning came into close conflict, and finally the Christian school took the place of the pagan university. The catechetical, or Socratic, element prevailed at first. The most active period of this school covered two centuries, A.D. 200–400. Pantænus was the founder. He and Clement stood at its head in the second century; Origen, Heracles, and Dionysius, in the third; and Didymus the Blind, in the fourth. In addition to these we may reckon Gregory Thaumaturgus, Petrus, Pamphilus, and Eusebius, who, though not formally connected with it, yet sympathized with its tendencies. The theological characteristics were sympathy with the better Greek philosophy, an emphasis on intuition and the subjective life, and a disposition to allegorize the Old-Testament narratives. Origen, though brilliant, was an unsafe guide, especially in his adoption of an eternal creation, the soul's pre-existence, a pre-adamite apostasy, and a final universal restoration.

4. **The School of Asia Minor** consisted less in a formal educational centre than in a group of theological writers and teachers. The whole region had been a scene of active theological thought since Paul's day. In the second century it leaned towards a literal and Judaistic type of Christianity, but in the third it assumed a broader character. It opposed Gnosticism and suppressed Montanism. Polycarp, Papias, Melito of Sardis, and

Hegesippus were its leaders in its first period; and Irenæus, Hippolytus, and Julius Africanus, in the second.

5. The School of Antioch, in Syria. Its chief pursuit was the criticism of the sacred text and the statement of doctrinal theology. Its founders were Dorotheus and Lukianus. At first it sympathized with the Alexandrian school, but was alienated on the rise of the Origenistic and Nestorian controversies. Its most prosperous period was A.D. 300–342. Theodorus, Eusebius of Emesa, Cyril, Apollinaris, Ephraem, Diodorus, John Chrysostom, and Theodore of Mopsuestia belonged to it.

6. The School of North Africa. Its centre was Carthage. To this place, and not to Rome, Latin Christianity was indebted for its prevailing type. Cyprian, Tertullian, Minutius Felix, Commodianus, and Arnobius were its leading representatives. It was distinguished for its heroic zeal for the unity of the Church, for aversion to Gnosticism, for an exact and literal Biblical interpretation, for an abhorrence of theological speculation, and for energy in developing the practical and evangelistic side of the Church. Its period of greatest prosperity was A.D. 200–330.

7. The General Tendency of the Schools was to lead the Church in its doctrinal and general literary development. They were rallying-points for Christian defence, and for broader plans of Christian work. Their influence extended throughout the Christian world. Many men were drawn towards them from the most distant regions, imbibed their spirit, and either went back as preachers and teachers into their own country, or far away, into new regions, to extend Christianity. Some of the teachers, as Origen, were of wonderfully magnetic spirit, and imparted both their energy and doctrines to younger minds.

Chapter XIII.

LIBERATION UNDER CONSTANTINE.

1. Political Life and the Church. We now come to consider the outward relations of the Church. What was the bearing of the empire upon Christianity? The period of persecution was passing away. The Church, meanwhile, was not despondent, but making full plans for future triumph. A revolution in the imperial policy was close at hand, and the forces were in full play which should soon bring about the liberation of all Christendom. This was effected by the military successes of Constantine, who, A.D. 306, was called from the command of the army in Britain to succeed his father as Roman emperor. But, before getting securely in place, he had to conquer five competitors—three in the East and two in the West. It mattered not that some were blood relatives. Kinship was only a trifle in those days, and soon Constantine had made way with all contestants to his claim to his father's crown.

2. Constantine declared himself a Christian, in sympathy, early in his reign. Before the decisive battle of the Rubra Saxa with Maxentius, which should secure his rule, he claimed to see in the sky the sign of the Cross, with the words "*En touto nika*"—"By this conquer." He accepted the token as an argument in favor of Christianity, gained the battle for the crown of the Roman Empire, and henceforth avowed his belief in

Christianity. His vision, though in the line of his sympathies, was probably only a shrewd method to attract the Christians to his support. He carried the labarum, a standard inscribed with the cross, in all his subsequent wars. His policy was at first to make all Christians the supporters of his rule, and, by granting concessions, to heal the alienation from the empire which the repressive policy of his predecessors had produced. He published (A.D. 313) an edict tolerating Christianity as one of the legal religions of the empire. But in the year 323 he enlarged the scope of his favor, and made Christianity the established faith of all his dominions.

THE LABARUM.

3. **The good and the bad in the imperial support.** It was a happy day when the Christians could walk abroad without fear of persecution. But there were grounds for concern. Constantine left but little for the Church to do for its own government. He claimed the right to supervise religion, as the emperor had always done in the case of paganism. He accounted himself still the great high-priest, or Pontifex Maximus, and claimed the prerogative to compose differences, decide questions of religious policy, call ecclesiastical councils, and appoint the leading officers. Then, again, he retained many pagan institutions. The heathen temples were supported out of the state treasury, certain respect was paid to the national divinities, and even soothsayers were still used for help in battle. Constantine was a mixed character, not willing to lose

the sympathy of the pagan citizens, and yet clear-headed enough to see that further hostility to Christianity would be fatal to his rule. He had no faith in paganism, but would not suppress it. His line of conduct was, to allow it to go on as he found it, and yet to help the Christians to conquer it. He was, of all successful rulers, the most successful trimmer.

4. The Danger to the Church. The course of Constantine was attended with serious danger to the Church. This did not arise from the assumption of guardianship over its affairs, but from making the whole Christian body a part of the machinery of the state, and employing the state as the supreme judge of its inner and outward life. Hitherto the Church had been a grand moral unity, held together by ties of love and doctrine. But now it was absorbed by the state. Its framework was lost in the body politic. Freeman says: "The Church conquered the state." This is a great error. Constantine's adoption of Christianity as the state religion was the conquest of the Church by the state. All the moral forces of the Church were now impaired. The bondage of the Church to the state, thus early begun, produced the great evils of the following twelve centuries—superstition, the purchase of office, the angry controversy about theological trifles, the moral corruption of the clergy, and the ignorance of the masses. Milton, in his translation of a passage of Dante's "Inferno," thus characterizes the evil of Constantine's favor:

> "Ah, Constantine, of how much ill was cause,
> Not thy conversion, but those rich demains
> That the first wealthy Pope received of thee!"

Charlemagne, and not Constantine, was the first to confer temporal power on the papacy. Dante was not far astray, however, for Constantine's patronage was the entering wedge for Charlemagne's donation. Neander says with truth: "The reign of Constantine bears witness that the state which seeks to establish Christianity by the worldly means at its command, may be the occasion of more injury to this holy cause than the earthly power which opposes it, with whatever force." Constantine could have helped the Church greatly by simply removing all political disabilities, and permitting the Christians to develop their polity and spiritual forces as God might lead.

5. Direct Favors to the Church. Among the chief special acts of Constantine in favor of the Church may be mentioned, his ordering the civil observance of Sunday, his confiscation in the East of pagan temples for Christian churches, his emancipation of the slaves, his exemption of the clergy from military and municipal duty, and his ardent promotion of Christian education among his subjects.

ST. SOPHIA, AT CONSTANTINOPLE.

Chapter XIV.

REACTION UNDER JULIAN.

1. The Three Sons of Constantine divided their father's empire among themselves. Not one was his equal, on the battle-field or in government. But they pursued his policy of favoring the Christian religion. The Christians were uncertain as to what would be the result when his immediate family should have passed away. The outlook was far from flattering. When Julian came to the throne there were grave apprehensions that he would renew the old war upon the Christians. For a time he was silent, but after a while he exhibited a spirit of refined opposition to all Christian institutions and doctrines.

2. Julian's Antecedents were calculated to prejudice his mind against Christianity. He was a nephew of Constantine, and was practically imprisoned in Cappadocia, because of supposed danger to the rule of Constantine's sons. He was educated in the languages and sciences, under the oversight of the Arian bishop, Eusebius, and was prepared for clerical service as a lector. But he regarded himself a victim of Christian persecution. In time he acquired liberty, by his brother Gallus becoming emperor in the East. He visited Constantinople, became acquainted with the pagan philosophy, and studied and adopted divination. On the death of Gallus (A.D. 354), he was carried a prisoner to Milan. On his release he went to Athens, and was initiated into the mysteries of Eleusis.

3. The Reign of Julian began A.D. 355. At first he shared the empire with Constantius, but on the latter's death he was declared by his soldiers the supreme ruler of the Roman Empire, on the bank of the Seine, where the Hôtel Clugny, the heart of old Paris, now stands. He early developed great military skill, and was successful in war. He here disappointed every one, for he had been supposed to be only a recluse, and a man of books. He regarded Constantine's family as fair Christian representatives, and hence he rejected Christianity, and revolutionized the imperial policy. He took up his abode in Constantinople, and adopted immediate measures to convert it into a pagan city. His one great object was to suppress Christianity, and restore paganism to its old grandeur, but with such improvements as might be derived from Oriental or any sources. He issued no formal edict against Christianity, but raised barriers on every hand. He claimed that his philosophy taught him toleration of all faiths. But this was a thin disguise. He was bitter towards the religion of Christ.

4. Julian's Opposition. The principal measures by which Julian sought to suppress Christianity were: 1, His encouragement of schism and strife among Christians; 2, the prohibition of Christian schools of learning and the study of classic authors by Christians, in the belief that Christianity could not exist without the classic basis; 3, his removal of disabilities from the Jews, and his proposed, but abortive, restoration of the temple at Jerusalem, that he might prove the falsity of Christ's prediction (Matt. xxiii. 38; xxiv. 2); 4, his requirement that the soldiers should attend heathen worship; 5, his withdrawal of existing immunities from the clergy; 6, his failure to punish his heathen subjects for deeds of violence against Christians; 7, his punishment of Christians for the slightest offences; his support of pagan services; and the rebuilding of the temples, at public expense; and, 8, his authorship of a work, now lost, in defence of paganism.

5. Death and Character. Julian's reign was short, lasting only twenty months. He died while on a campaign against the Persians (A.D. 363). It was currently believed by the Christians that his last words were: "*Tandem vicisti, Galilæa*"—"Thou, O Galilean, hast conquered, after all." He was a compound of elements not often found in one individual. He was fanatical in treatment of the Christians, shrewd in political plans, brilliant as a military commander, cultivated in all the learning of his age, vain in the extreme, and wildly superstitious. He not only believed that Christianity was sure to die, but that he was the destined instrument to kill it. He had the egotism to believe that he excelled in literary work, an infirmity for which royal authors have generally been distinguished. Like Frederick the Great, he was never so weak as with pen in hand. His proposed new eclectic religion was heterogeneous beyond description. It was a mixture of Neo-Platonic speculation, the arts of jugglery, the moralizings of Rome's best Stoic thinkers, and the wild dreams of Persian fire-worshippers. Here and there a grain of the golden truth of the Bible was dropped in, but not enough to cover the glaring shallowness of the general scheme. His god was the Mithra, or Sun-God of the East, beneath whom were numerous tutelary divinities, derived from Grecian paganism and Alexandrian gnosticism. His methods of rehabilitating paganism were on the Christian plan. He re-established the priesthood on the basis of the Christian ministry; his pagan bishops preached to the people, and expounded the pagan mythologies; he foisted into pagan use the constitution of the Church; provided for penance, excommunication, absolution, and restoration; twisted Christian psalmody into the heathen rites, where choirs chanted and congregations responded, after the most approved ecclesiastical mode; and provided hospitals for the sick, destitute, and orphans, and gave alms after the manner of the Christian diaconate. But all failed. Even an emperor could not mix Christianity and paganism. He was the last ruler on the Roman throne who was hostile to Christianity. He passed into history as Julian the Apostate. The epithet is probably a misapplication, as it is not likely that Julian was ever anything else than an enemy to Christianity.

CHAPTER XV.

THE MONTANISTIC REFORM.

1. Reaction against Loose Discipline. During the persecutions of the first three centuries some of the Christians relapsed into paganism. A portion of these afterwards regretted their apostasy, and wished to return to the Church, and be received as penitents. Within the Church there prevailed two sentiments concerning them—a lax view, which exacted but little more of the penitent than a pledge of future fidelity; and a severe view, which kept the applicant for readmission on a long probation, and, in many instances, would not receive him at all. These two views, however, took a wider range than the readmission of the lapsed into the Church. The imperial favor was already bringing in disorders of many kinds. Many Christians, both East and West, protested against them, while the more wealthy saw no real danger to vital Christianity by making certain social concessions. The former and stricter class found expression in the life and career of Montanus, a native Phrygian.

2. The Plan of Montanism. Montanus, like the people among whom he was reared, was fond of the marvellous and ecstatic. The old national worship was that of Cybele, who was here honored as nowhere else. Divination and clairvoyance were believed to be priestly endowments. Political disaster only fanned the flame of devotion to Cybele. In time, Christianity made its way among the people, and here grew up some of those churches of Asia, such as Laodicea and Colosse, to which John addressed epistles. But the natural temperament remained undisturbed, and the people carried into Christianity the same firm fidelity to their new faith which they had entertained towards paganism. The followers of Montanus demanded a return to the apostolical life of the Church. He had been a priest of Cybele, and, when he became a Christian, he was as warm for his new faith as he had been for his old one. There was not a trace of idolatry left in him; but his nature was quite the same. He remained the visionary and the prophet. He proposed to regenerate the life of all Christendom. He saw departures from the old simplicity and purity, which he regarded himself as the chosen instrument for removing. His place, therefore, was that of the reformer. It was an obscure region to produce a man of such superior claims. But he stood out before the whole Christian world as the representative of the old and pure faith.

3. The Opinions of Montanus. He combined the practical and visionary to a remarkable degree. He claimed that there are three persons in the Godhead: Father, Son, and Spirit, and that through himself the third person, the Paraclete, prophesied to the world. The world will speedily end, and then the millennial reign of Christ will begin. The real Church is the pure Church. Nothing but absolute purity must be allowed in it. There is a universal priesthood of believers. Penitence must take place after sin, but sacrificing again to idols should exclude from total restoration to the Church. But God may still forgive.

4. The Expansion of Montanism went rapidly on. Communities sprang up, not in Phrygia alone, but in many other regions. They were small societies in the general Church—*ecclesiolæ in ecclesia*—like the Pietistic organizations within the bosom of the German Protestant Church, in the seventeenth century. The bishop, Julianus, tried to win them back, but, failing, adopted severer methods. Two councils were held, at both of which the Montanists were condemned.

Rome favored their cause at first, but afterwards settled down into a sentiment of firm opposition. The looser discipline of the Western Christians was not likely to harmonize with it. But in Gaul there was a close sympathy, where the bonds between the Christians and those of Asia Minor had always been very close. In North Africa the views of Montanus gained new favor and great prestige, through the support of Tertullian. He advocated the universal necessity of a stricter discipline, and eliminated some of the vagaries of original Montanism. His name gave it new respectability; but, with even this great advantage, the system was doomed. The condemnation by the councils; the visionary speculations of Montanus; and the prominence of ecstasy, vision, and chiliasm in the movement, were as millstones about its neck. Its stronger qualities were overlooked in the vigorous warfare upon it. The episcopacy found it an inconvenient thing, as its tendency was to curtail the episcopal prerogative. Montanism was bitterly opposed to all centralization of authority. The Roman emperors opposed it everywhere. At last it disappeared, even in Phrygia, and was found only in a sect in North Africa, bearing the name Tertullianists. Justinian issued two edicts against Montanism, A.D. 530–532, after which it sank beneath the waves of more exciting questions.

CHAPTER XVI.

CONTROVERSIES ON CHRIST.

1. The Arian Strife. The principal scene of this important controversy was Alexandria, Palestine, and Constantinople. The question was concerning the divinity of Christ. Both Jews and pagans very early united in opposing this doctrine, believing that it was vital to the Christians. John's gospel, the inspired apology, proves how early our Lord's divine character was assailed. Later, there came, as accessories towards a low Christological view, the vague teachings of the Antiochian school and the incongruities of the theology of Origen. The period during which the controversy lasted is divided into two parts — A.D. 318 - 361 and 361–381. Arius was a presbyter of Alexandria. He derived his theological ideas from the Antiochian school, which emphasized the unity of the divine nature, and looked with great alarm on any doctrine which would seem to destroy it.

2. The Outbreak in Alexandria took place A.D. 318. Alexander, bishop of Alexandria, advocated the eternal Sonship of Christ, and his equality with the Father. Arius opposed him, holding that there was a time when the Son did not exist; that, having a beginning, he can not be of the same essence with the Father; that he was a creature, and not Creator; that he was divinely illumined, and therefore the Logos; that he is subordinate to the Father, and that the Holy Ghost is subordinate to the Son. The issue was clearly defined. For a time Alexandria was the sole scene of the controversy, and the participants were the bishop and his presbyter. Alexander called a synod in Alexandria, when Arius was deposed. But violent opposition arose to this summary dealing with a man of the pure life of Arius. The scene now widened. Constantine, the emperor, ordered the contestants to stop the quarrel. But no attention was paid to the command. The strife raged with increased bitterness. When the emperor was informed by Hosius, bishop of Cordova, whom he had sent as a special messenger to Alexandria, to inquire into the state of affairs, that the controversy was no trifling matter, and would not cease at a mere order, he convened a council.

3. The Council of Nicæa, A.D. 325. This was the most important assembly of the early Church. It was attended by representatives from every part of Christendom. Even India sent its bishop. There were about three hundred bishops, besides many of the inferior clergy. Constantine arrived during the session, and presided over the deliberations. Athanasius stood at the head of the orthodox party. The result of the council was the condemnation of Arius and the passing of the celebrated Nicene creed. Arius now became an exile in Illyria. Constantine, influenced by the persuasions of certain bishops, but particularly by the entreaties of Constantia, widow of the Emperor Licinius, invited Arius to his court, ordered Athanasius to receive him back into the Church, and threatened deposition and banishment in case of refusal. Athanasius replied, that he could not acknowledge as Christian those whom the whole Church had condemned. The emperor then ceased his importunities. But the Arians made Constantine believe that Athanasius was a political enemy, charging him with preventing the sailing of the Egyptian fleet with supplies for Constantinople. He was thereupon banished to Treves, in Gaul, A.D. 336.

4. The Fortunes of Arianism. The subsequent history of Arian opinions was checkered. Athanasius and Arius stood before the Christian world as the representatives of orthodoxy and heterodoxy. The changes in imperial sympathy were frequent, the Arians enjoying quite as much the sunshine of the palace as their orthodox adversaries. The general council of Sardica, in Illyria, A.D. 343, renewed the conclusions of Nicæa. But Arian opinions still gained ground in the East, while in the West the opposition was only tacit and negative. When Julian gained the throne he recalled Athanasius from exile, but afterwards banished him again. That ruler was ready for any measure by which Christians could be pitted against each other. The council of Constantinople, A.D. 381, condemned the Arians once more, and two years later the Emperor Theodosius issued an edict against them. In the remoter parts of the empire they gained strength. Some of the ruder tribes adopted their view. Ulfilas was a Gothic bishop of Arian views. The celebrated Codex Argenteus, now preserved in the University of Upsala, Sweden, was his translation of the four Gospels into the Mæso-Gothic language of the end of the fourth century. The Vandals and Moors of North Africa became Arians, but were conquered, because of a rebellion during the reign of Justinian. Gradually the heresy disappeared alike from the centres and the outlying provinces. By the end of the sixth century the only Arian people left were the Lombards, of Italy.

Chapter XVII.

THE LATER CONTROVERSIES.

1. The New Issues were largely related to the person of Christ. The Arian strife turned entirely upon his divine nature, but questions connected directly with this doctrine arose, which absorbed universal attention, and continued long after the Arian controversy had ceased to divide the Christian world. These new issues related to the person of Christ in his incarnate existence. The singular characteristic of these collateral controversies, which were separate currents flowing out of the Arian fountain, lies in the fact that they became permanent factors in the Church. For, from them have come the present Coptic and Nestorian churches, with some smaller subdivisions of Oriental Christianity.

2. Apollinarism. Apollinaris believed that the prevalent Christian view of the two natures in Christ savored of both Judaism and paganism. He held that the divine Logos first attained a personal existence in the man Jesus; that full divinity and humanity in one were impossible; that Christ's humanity was eternally complete; and that the human is only the organ for revealing the divine. By ignoring the essential features of our Lord's humanity, and involving it with the divine to such an extent that it became a mixed essence, Apollinaris subjected himself to the charge of heresy. His opinions were condemned by the councils of Rome, A.D. 377 and 378; by the council of Constantinople, A.D. 381; and by the imperial decrees, A.D. 388, 397, and 428. Apollinaris withdrew from the Church in A.D. 375, and died A.D. 390.

3. Nestorianism. This controversy raged over a broad territory, and excelled all others of the time in its vigorous vitality, and its power to project itself into the later ages. It was another product of the restless and inventive Antioch. Nestorius became bishop of Constantinople, A.D. 428. He saw the danger of Arianism, and, in his zeal to defend the full divinity of our Lord, went so far as to do injustice to his humanity. He went beyond Apollinaris, and yet was in a measure of sympathy with the Pelagians, because of the total absence of fatalism in their system and the large place which they gave to the freedom of the will. His opinions were, that Christ possessed two natures, the divine and human; that there are not two persons, however, but only one; that there is a perfect union between the perfect God, the Word, and man, which is expressed by the word *sunapheia* (conjunction); that the divine so far transcends the human as largely to absorb it; and that God the Son did not endure human suffering, or go through human experiences. Instead of regarding Christ as the God-man, Nestorius held that he was the God-bearing man. The body of our Lord was simply the vehicle of the divine, the temple of the Logos. These views attracted profound attention. They were advocated with so much warmth and ability, not only by Nestorius, but by many who rallied to his support, that they spread with marvellous rapidity, and extended from the shores of the Ægean Sea to the boundaries of India. They were condemned by several councils. The Emperor Zeno (A.D. 489) dissolved the Nestorian school of Edessa, and hoped in this way to arrest the heresy. But here he failed. It was a system which could live without a theology. The Nestorians can still be found, even in name as well as doctrines, in Koordistan and the valley of the Tigris and Euphrates. Humboldt bears witness to their contributions to the arts and sciences in the East, while their schools and hospitals have been of benign influence through all the intervening centuries.

4. **Augustine**, born in Tagaste, Numidia, A.D. 354, was led to adopt Christianity while young through the example of his devout mother, Monica. He afterwards became worldly, and wandered far from the principles and example of his early life. When thirty-two years of age he was restored to a pure and happy state, and was baptized by the aged Ambrose, Bishop of Milan. His mother, who never lost faith in him, and who had followed him in all his wanderings over many lands, had the great joy of witnessing his restoration to the Church. He became a presbyter in Africa, A.D. 399, was elected bishop of Hippo Regius, in Numidia, and died there A.D. 430. The theology of Augustine was as follows: Man was created pure, in God's image, and possessed of a free will. He was tempted and fell, and in him all humanity sinned. But man was capable of restoration, not of himself, but of God's grace. This grace comes not because man believes, but precedes faith, and is given that he may believe. From this grace all the stages of repentance, conversion, and final perseverance are reached and passed through. Now, as grace is a free gift of God, and precedes all acts of faith on man's part, and as experience shows that not all men become converted and are saved, it must follow that God absolutely predestinates a cer-

COUNTRY of the NESTORIANS.

tain number to salvation (*decretum absolutum*), and that the rest are left to their merited damnation. There were many departments of this new system, and Augustine defended them all with fervor and logical skill. His purity of life and noble character added great force to his theology.

5. The Pelagian Controversy. Out of the Augustinian theology sprang the Pelagian controversy. It marked the entrance of the Anglo-Saxon into the broad domain of the general theology of the Christian Church. Pelagius was a monk of Britain, who resided in Rome, and about A.D. 409 began to propagate his doctrines. He attacked the Augustinian system on every side. He controverted the innate depravity of man, and held that man was created mortal; that Adam's fall has made no change in human nature, and has exerted no influence on his posterity; that the heart is a *tabula rasa*, or blank, and has no inclination to virtue or vice; that man's will is perfectly free to choose virtue or vice; that Christ became man, not to save by his atoning blood, but to aid us by his doctrine and example to attain to everlasting life; that baptism is a necessity; and that children dying unbaptized reach a lower grade of salvation than the baptized.

6. The Spread of the Controversy. Pelagius succeeded while in Rome in winning to his doctrines the acute and learned Cœlestius. Both were of pure life and ascetic tastes. They went to Africa, A.D. 411, and afterwards Pelagius proceeded to Palestine, while Cœlestius remained in Africa, and became a presbyter. The deacon Paulinus opposed the Pelagian system, and became a strong aid to Augustine. In Palestine it encountered a strong opponent in Hieronymus, but the synod of Jerusalem (A.D. 415) declined to condemn the doctrines of Pelagius, and intimated that the whole controversy was a Western affair, and was of no special concern to Eastern Christians. The African Church, however, took up the question, and the two synods of Mileve and Carthage (A.D. 416) condemned the Pelagians. An appeal was made by Pelagius to the Roman bishop, Innocent I., but the latter died before it reached him. His successor, Zosimus, espoused the Pelagian cause, and wrote an endorsement to Africa. But a new synod was called in Carthage (A.D. 417), which confirmed the former action against Pelagius. The Roman Emperor, Honorius, now took part in the strife, and banished the Pelagians from Rome. This brought Zosimus to drop his Pelagianism, and he wrote a circular letter against it. Suddenly the scene of controversy was shifted to the East, with Constantinople as the centre. The third general council of the Church was held in Ephesus, A.D. 431, and Pelagius and Cœlestius were condemned, at the same time with Nestorius. The controversy assumed a milder type, later, in the West, under the name of semi-Pelagianism. The sharpness of both Augustinism and Pelagianism was toned down. The result was the triumph of a mild type of the Augustinian theology, adopted by the synod of Aranico (Orange), A.D. 529.

7. **Other Controversies** grew out of these larger ones. Each district had its own views, while individual communities were distinguished for their espousal of some leader, which meant bitter hostility against his competitor. There was no want of hair-splitting. The philosophical terms of the Greek schools, which it was thought were dead, again came to life, and were hurled with energy from man to man and land to land. "*Theotokos*"—"God born"—a word used by Nesto-

rius, was heard from Gaul and Italy to the borders of modern Thibet and India. All Christendom was divided by a single letter of the alphabet, one half crying "Homoiousia" (like essence), and the other half responding with equal fervor, "Homoousia" (same essence). Gregory of Nazianzus bears the following witness to the extent to which the theological discussions pervaded all classes. "The city (Constantinople) is full of people, who dogmatize on incomprehensible questions. The streets and market-places are the scenes of discussions of the old-clothes dealers, the money changers, and the venders of green-groceries. If you ask how many *oboli* he asks for his produce, he will respond by dogmatizing on the Begotten and the Unbegotten. If you inquire the price of bread, you will get for answer, 'The Father is greater than the Son, and the Son is subordinate to the Father.' If you inquire, 'Is the bath ready?' you will hear, 'The Son was created from nothing.'"

8. **The Results of the Agitations** were, on the whole, favorable to Christianity. At the moment they must have seemed not only fruitless, but of infinite damage. This is always the judgment of the age which produces theological discussions. Controversy seems only evil when in progress. But, judged by later generations, one sees the good results. The agitations of the apostolic period, and of the four centuries succeeding it, aroused the Christians to a sense of the importance of formulating their doctrines. They were led to meet in great councils, to compare views, and lay down those creeds, one by one, which have served the purpose of doctrinal statement for all later ages. The masses were brought to examine the Scriptures with great care, and to see how far the prevailing doctrines were supported

by them. The average Christian was led to distinguish between truth and error, and to perceive the vast danger which came, in a rude age, from propagating falsehood. It was a time of test. The furnace was at a white heat. Every truth which lay at the foundation of Christianity was subjected to the flames. The pagans from without had attempted, by their attacks, to destroy Christianity. But, in the period of controversy, the Christians examined their whole body of truth with their own hands. They now gave proof that they could discuss together with as much animation as against their common foe. The Council of Nicæa, A.D. 325, which determined the divinity of Christ, and that of Chalcedon, A.D. 451, which determined the union of the two natures in him, undisturbed and unmixed, made immortal statements. Hence, even in the midst of the controversial period, we can easily see positive advances of the cause of Christianity.

Chapter XVIII.

ECCLESIASTICAL SCHISMS.

1. The Schism of Felicissimus. Division in the Church was intimately connected with the controversies. But the formal secessions did not arise so much from differences of opinions in theological speculation as in practical life. Felicissimus was the originator of an important schism, which extended from Carthage to the shores of the Atlantic. Cyprian, the Bishop of Carthage, had dealt leniently with the lapsed who sought readmission to the Church. Felicissimus took the stricter view, and opposed Cyprian, first, on the basis of the alleged irregular method of the latter's election to the episcopacy, and then because of his mild measures in restoring the lapsed into the favor of the Church.

2. The Novatian Schism, A.D. 251, was produced by Novatianus, with Rome as the scene. The origin lay in the corrupt measures by which Callistus, after many adventures, arrived in Rome, and secured election to the episcopacy. He granted absolution to all the excommunicated alike. He permitted a second marriage, and even a third, to his clergy. After his death the lax party continued in force. In A.D. 251 the presbyter Cornelius was chosen bishop, and his methods were similar to those of his predecessor. Novatianus, a presbyter, opposed him with great spirit. He claimed that the Church consisted of the pure only; that there could be no chaff among the good wheat. An important secession was the outcome, with Novatianus as leader. It extended into the East, and in Phrygia received strong support. It lost strength, however, with the death of its leader, and in time went into decay.

3. **The Donatist Schism** arose from the same general cause as the other separatistic movements. But it involved more serious questions, assumed larger proportions, continued longer, and made a more thorough encroachment on the life and organization of the Church than any previous schism. It began with the question of the practical religious life, but soon extended into the domain of ecclesiastical discipline, and then entered the larger sphere of the relation of the Church to the state. In North Africa the spirit of martyrdom, during the persecutions, assumed, in many cases, the form of a monomania. Christians, in large numbers, thought that by voluntary death they could atone for all former errors. Fanaticism took the place of a calm and resigned submission to the inevitable. Then came reverence for the bones of the martyrs, and for the places of their death. Many Christians thought they saw in special places and relics the abode of sanctity and the source of blessings. The question now became of such interest that elections to the episcopal office turned upon fancies arising out of this fanatical spirit. Donatus, a Numidian bishop, appeared at Carthage, opposed the election of Cæcilian as bishop on the ground that he had been consecrated by Felix, a traditor, or renouncer of the Scriptures, in the time of persecution. Donatus stood at the head of the stricter party, and would surrender nothing to the more lax Christians. The entire Church of North Africa was involved in the strife. From words the difference went so far as

secession. A council at Arles, in France, condemned the Donatists. But they had warm supporters, and bore persecution firmly. In the year 321 the Emperor Constantine issued a special edict, granting them full religious liberty. For twenty years they had peace, during which time they built churches, organized societies, built up a vast ecclesiastical system, and were represented by their own bishop in the Nicene council. After the death of Donatus the sect divided into extremists and moderates. In course of time the schism lost its hold upon the favor of the people, and disappeared.

4. The Meletian Schism. During the Diocletian persecution, when Peter was metropolitan of Alexandria, and Meletius was bishop of Lycopolis, in the Thebaid, the latter took advantage of the retirement of the former to ordain ministers in dioceses outside his own. He complained that, as many bishops were absent, the Church was suffering from want of their services. The bishops who were in captivity remonstrated against his course. Meletius held to the stricter view, and Epiphanius reports that Meletius was the representative of the stricter party in the Church. An Egyptian synod took measures against Meletius, and condemned him, for assuming functions not belonging to him. The schism extended over all Egypt, and was not without powerful support in other regions. Twenty-nine Meletian bishops were present at the Council of Nicæa. But the schism itself was condemned, though in mild terms. After the council Meletius continued his schismatic course, but without real success. He afterwards combined with the Arians. After the middle of the fifth century the Meletians disappeared from history.

Chapter XIX.

THE SCRIPTURES AND TRADITION.

1. The Old-Testament Canon. The need of a fixed and complete canon of revealed truth was felt by the Church in its earliest period. As to just what writings were canonical, the authority rested first with the Jews. Of these there were two classes—the more exact and literal, who lived in Palestine, and preserved most fully the traditions of their ancestors; and the more free and inexact, who lived in Alexandria, and were inclined to permit doubtful books to enter the recognized canon. The Christians looked to the Palestinian Jews as the safer guides, and hence modelled their canon on the more conservative plan. The need of the Scriptures, and of knowing precisely what constituted the canon, was pressed upon the early Church with great force. The apologists heard from all sides the bitter lament, "You are divided as to your sacred books! Tell us what they are!" Hence, every safe means was employed to get at uniformity. Some Christian teachers were inclined to admit doubtful books. For example: Origen defended the narrative of Susanna against the attack of Julius Africanus; he was equally energetic in his plea for Tobit and Judith. Barnabas declared the four books of Ezra to be inspired. Tertullian attached the same value to the Book of Enoch. Hermas elevated to similar honor the Book of Eldam and Modal, two men whom tradition alleged to have written a prophecy in the wilderness. Melito, bishop of Sardis, visited Palestine (A.D. 170), with a view to getting at the best understanding concerning the Jewish view of the real canon. It may be safely said that, by the beginning of the second century, there was a general understanding among Christians as to the exact books of the Old-Testament canon. They are the same which the evangelical Protestant Church of our times regards as inspired.

2. The New Testament. There was more hesitation and uncertainty in arriving at agreement on the New-Testament canon. The whole period of the early Church was one of intense literary fertility. Many books were written by Christians which the average believer had loved so dearly, and which had been so helpful, that it is not surprising he should place them closely beside the works of Paul and John. The Epistle of Barnabas, Clement's Epistle to the Corinthians, Polycarp's Epistle to the Philippians, the Shepherd of Hermas, the Gospel of the Hebrews, and the Apocalypse of Peter, had each its friends. The Muratori fragment, which proceeded from the Roman or North African Church, gives the first list of canonical books:—the Gospels, the Acts of the Apostles, thirteen epistles by Paul, the first epistle of John, and the first epistle of Peter. As early as A.D. 170 these were accepted as the canon, but with a general belief that time would show it necessary to make the list larger. There was a difference of sentiment, according to the country, and even the community. The second and third epistles of John, and the Apocalypse, were in general, but not universal, use, for the Peshito is the only collection omitting them. Jude was accepted by the great body of the Church, but James was admitted by the Syrians only. Greek and Syrian Christians admitted the epistle to the Hebrews, but the Western Church repelled it. Second Peter was longer in dispute than any of the New-Testament writings. Origen and Eusebius declared against it; but other teachers were equally warm in their advocacy.

3. Settlement of the Whole Canon. The Christian scholars were not inclined to hasten towards a conclusion. They were not willing to decide in one century what a more thorough scholarship in the next would make it necessary to revoke. But in time they reached a general understanding. The East and the West combined their views, and found that, after all, there was an identity of opinion. By the end of the fourth century there was a general understanding as to the proper books to be classed as the canon. Nothing now remained but to declare this exact canon. This was done by the Synod of Hippo, in North Africa, A.D. 393, under the leadership of Augustine. This list of the inspired books comprised our present twenty-seven books of the New Testament. The Council of Carthage, A.D. 397, adopted the same resolution. Shortly afterwards, Innocent, Bishop of Rome, gave his approval to the conclusions of the councils of Hippo and Carthage. From this time forth, for eleven centuries, there was no change in the sentiment of the Church as to its canonical Scriptures. The Council of Trent, which met A.D. 1545, to promote the interests of the Roman Catholic Church, against the new and vigorous Protestantism, was the first great body to elevate the Apocrypha into equal honor with those other books of the Old Testament which have never been questioned.

4. The Force of Tradition. In a time when the copies of the Scriptures were only in manuscript, and of great cost, much value was attached to the personal recollections of the apostles and their immediate successors. Tradition, or matter handed down from father to son, was rich in reminiscence, and not likely, for two or three centuries, to go very far astray from exact history. That the narratives of aged Christians, which they had heard many years before from their seniors, should possess great interest to the societies where they belonged, and were soon to die, is not surprising. There is a rich glow and delightful fragrance in the words of Irenæus to Florin, in which he repeats what he had heard, when very young, from the lips of the aged Polycarp, who had been taught when young by John, and who had told him much of what the beloved disciple had repeated concerning the miracles, doctrines, and life of our Lord. Irenæus thus continues: "This I, Irenæus, too, heard, at that time, with all eagerness, and wrote down, not on parchment, but in my heart, and, by God's grace, I constantly bring it up again to remembrance."

5. **The Later Tradition,** as understood many centuries afterwards, and playing an important part in the faith of Christian people, carried with it three elements: Apostolic origin, catholicity, and communication by the bishops. But the early tradition was simply the unwritten truth, and orally communicated from one generation to another. It was never, at this early period, clothed with any such force as belonged to the Scriptures. Origen and Irenæus went further than most teachers in the large place they gave to tradition. But theirs was not the prevailing view in the Church. Tradition was regarded a treasure of priceless value, because preserving the golden links by which the *memorabilia* of the apostles and companions of our

Lord were treasured. But there was no tendency to raise tradition to equality with the Scriptures, much less to lift it above them. This unhistorical and unjust view was never originated until the sixteenth century; nor assumed form until the syncretistic controversy of the seventeenth century; nor was made an argument against the orthodoxy and scholarship of the early Church until the eighteenth, when Semler and Lessing found it serviceable to build up a theory. The precise relation of Scripture and tradition in the early Church was one of friendly, but not equal, juxtaposition. No tradition of the period had the confidence of the general body of believers which was not based upon, and in harmony with, the Scriptures. So far as doctrine was concerned, tradition was simply that unwritten construction of doctrine which afterwards assumed fixed form in the great symbols of the Church.

Chapter XX.

APOCRYPHAL WRITINGS.

1. The Inventive Spirit of the early Church can be fully seen in the large mass of apocryphal works. While the close of the Scriptural canon sealed the fate of all such writings, there was still a strong local attachment to some of them. One of the chief sources of these apocryphal productions was the Ebionitic and Gnostic heresies. The great body of the Church was busied in resisting these heresies, and yet the Ebionites and Gnostics themselves produced many such works, and to the great outlying world the Christian Church had to bear the responsibility for the authorship of works produced by its own heretics.

2. The Broad Field. The authors of the spurious writings confined themselves to no narrow territory. The whole realm of thought lay open to them, and they roamed at large. They were as much at home in the patriarchal times as in later periods, and were as skilful in writing works in the name of the Roman Clement as of Paul or Isaiah. The five favorite fields were: 1. Old-Testament history; 2. The life of Jesus; 3. The life and labors of the apostles; 4. The Epistles; and, 5. Ecclesiastical polity and discipline.

3. Particular Books. The Book of Enoch enjoyed large popularity. It was a product of the century immediately preceding Christ, but in the second century it underwent adaptations to the new Christian conditions. It has been preserved in a translation from the Ethiopic MS. The Testimony of the Twelve Patriarchs, written by a Jewish Christian, contains prophecy and admonition. It claims to have been written by the twelve sons of Jacob, who instruct their posterity on various duties, and foretell our Lord's incarnation and the downfall of Judaism. The Apocalypse of Moses, Isaiah's Ascension to Heaven, the Fourth Book of Ezra, and the Prophecies of Hystaspes belong in the same prophetic category.

4. **The Sibylline Oracles.** These were in fourteen books, and were in imitation of the Roman Sibyllines, which enjoyed wide popularity. The Christian Sibyllines were designed to promote Christian interests. They were prophecies concerning the second coming of Christ, the destruction of Rome, the coming of Nero as antichrist, and the final triumph of Christianity. The Christian apologists made frequent appeals to them, though with varying confidence. They claim, in the text, to have been written by a daughter-in-law of Noah. This was certainly far enough back to satisfy the most antiquarian taste of the times.

5. **The Apocryphal Accounts of Our Lord** were abundant. The First Gospel of James the Less was a minute description of the alleged early life of Christ, and of the personal history of Mary. The Gospel of the Nativity of St. Mary, the History of Joachim and Anna, and of the Birth of Mary and the Infant Saviour, the History of Joseph the Carpenter, the Gospel of the Infant Saviour, and the Gospel of Thomas, furnished a vast mass of legendary matter, which, though worse than valueless, shows at least how profoundly the thought of the Church was centred in the life and person of Jesus. The Gospel of Nicodemus, the Acts

of Pilate, and the Epistles of Lentulus bear on the Passion of our Lord, and are very minute in legendary details. To the spurious apostolical correspondence belong the Epistle of Barnabas, the Epistle to the Laodiceans, an Epistle to the Corinthians, in the Armenian language, the correspondence of Paul with Seneca, the Epistle of Ignatius to the Mother of Jesus, and the Epistles of the Holy Virgin to the inhabitants of Messina, Florence, and other cities. The Apocalypse of Peter, the Ascension of Paul, and the Apocalypses of Thomas and Stephen, and a second one by John, are only a small portion of this luxuriant department of spurious Christian literature.

6. The Apostolical Constitutions. This is the most important writing on discipline and order proceeding from the early Church. It is a collection of eight books of instruction for both the clergy and laity on practical duties and ecclesiastical usages and polity. They claim to have been written by the apostles, but really arose at different times, no part having existed earlier than the third century. The first six books bear internal evidence of having been written in the last quarter of the third century, while the seventh and eighth indicate an origin not earlier than the fourth century. The Apostolic Canons are brief rules for ecclesiastical discipline and law. They were issued by the Roman Clement as an authentic work of the apostles, but were afterwards declared by the Roman bishop Hormisdas, in the sixth century, to be apocryphal. The second Trullan Council, A.D. 692, recognized them as authority for the Eastern Church.

Chapter XXI.

THEOLOGY DURING THE EARLY PERIOD.

1. General Agreement. On the fundamental Christian doctrines there was a general agreement among Christians, both East and West, even before the first formula of truth was established: namely, by the Council of Nicæa, A.D. 325. There was a bold discussion of great themes. The daring of those first heroes for the truth is astounding. With only a brief history, and writhing in the agonies of martyrdom, they nevertheless wrote on themes of the broadest character. There was a difference between the Greek and Roman Christian. The Greek was speculative. He caught up the terminology of Aristotle and the rest, and thrust it boldly into his argument on the eternal generation of our Lord. There was no subject on which he did not enter with boundless enthusiasm. The Roman was more careful. He had less to say, but more to do. He went beyond his pile of manuscripts, and thought of a stronger organization of the Church, a firmer body of believers, a more solid Christian phalanx for the conquest of the world. But, beneath the speculation of the Greek and the practical aggressiveness of the Roman, there was one faith. With all the differences in the schools, there was but little difference in the ruling theology.

2. The Divine Character lay at the foundation of all doctrine. Here the Christian mind came into severest antagonism to the Greek polytheism and the Oriental dualism. The Christian believer regarded God as Creator and Preserver of the universe. No attribute in modern evangelical theology was denied him in the patristic period. Only when the Christians began to consider the relations of the three persons in the Godhead, and God's revelation of himself to the world, do we observe variety. But even here there was essential unity. Tertullian varied from the general view in supposing God must have a body. This he did because of the misfortune of his philosophy, which was borrowed from paganism, that corporeity is a necessity of all existence. Origen and the school of Alexandria controlled the Church in avoiding all corporeal representations of deity. The whole patristic Church said, "We accept the divine character. We do not need to prove it. Its proof is in us and beyond us." Arnobius said, "To attempt to prove God's existence is not much better than to deny it." Origen, Clement of Alexandria, and Athanasius agreed in saying that the only possible knowledge we can have of God is based on grace and the Logos.

3. **Unity and Trinity.** The methods of proving these attributes of the Godhead were not fortunate. Instead of adhering to the language of the Scriptures, the theologians made use, as well, of the dialectics of Aristotle, and of the example of the elder faiths of India and of Persia, to show a parallelism. Yet there was no compromise; no disposition to reduce the Christian doctrine to the plane of any other faith. The term *triad* was first used by Theophilus of Antioch, while Tertullian was the first to introduce the word *trinity* into Christian theology. While all the fathers accepted the three persons, there was a difference of method in proving the equality of essence.

Justin's view expressed, however, the general and final belief of the Church: The three persons exist; they are of equal quality; beneath all the variety in the universe there is a unity of operation by the one God.

4. Christology. This was the most fully developed of all departments of theology. The Logos of Alexandria became the Logos of the Christian world. Some teachers proved the incarnation of our Lord by a process of necessity; that to reveal is a divine necessity, just as the gem must shine. But this was a low plane of logic. The prevailing method was: God is all-loving and all-wise, and he willed the salvation of man, and by the only means possible. God's nature is to bless. He is not an introspective character. His goodness is operative when it is needed. It was the Father's good pleasure to reveal himself. His will absorbed all necessity. Our Lord was generated by the Holy Ghost, born of the Virgin Mary, and led a human life. This life was sinless. Justin, Theophilus of Antioch, Tatian, and the pseudo-Ignatius held that the Son existed from all eternity coequally with the Father, but that, before creation, he proceeded from the Father, and began to lead a separate personal existence. Irenæus taught Christ's separate and personal Sonship with the Father; Tertullian, that the members of the Trinity are of the same substance, but constitute a succession; and Origen, that the Logos was of eternal generation. There was a gradual approach to unity of view, which was finally crystallized in the statement of Nicæa. The Christian thinkers had been in danger, on the one hand, of emphasizing the humanity of our Lord to the detriment of his divinity; and, on the other, of allowing his divinity to absorb his humanity. But the perfection of each nature finally entered into the permanent faith of the Church. The final Christology of the period reduces itself to this: Christ was eternally coexistent and co-operative with the Father; he permitted the full penalty of sin to be visited upon himself; his death was voluntary, and achieved our redemption; he rose from the dead, ascended into heaven, became our High Priest; in the fulness of time he will come to judge the world, when he will reward the righteous and punish the guilty.

5. The Holy Spirit. The discussions on the Logos threw the consideration of the Holy Ghost into the background. The adversaries of Christianity knew that Christianity must stand or fall with the divinity of Christ. There was no emphatic and general discussion of the doctrine of the Holy Ghost before the fourth century. This, however, must not be regarded as an early doubt of the divine character and personality of the third person in the Trinity, as alleged by the Tübingen school. On the contrary, it was a doctrine so firmly accepted that the defence of it was not considered a necessity. Later, the separate and divine personality of the Holy Ghost, with all his divine offices, was clearly laid down by Origen and Tertullian, and was formally laid down in the conclusions of the general councils.

6. Cosmology. Here was a fruitful field of speculation. "Is matter eternal?" was a question which Persia had hurled at the Western mind, and because Christianity answered "No," the whole Oriental philosophy opposed the new religion. The Christian claimed that his sacred books taught that only an eternal God could create matter. Tertullian spoke for the whole Church when he said, that God did not need the world for his own glory, but that creation was for man.

7. Anthropology. The pagan believed in a past golden age. The Christian looked back upon lost Paradise, but his eye was keen to foresee a perfect restoration. He studied man in relation to the future. Sin passed from our first parents upon all humanity. Theophilus of Antioch and Tertullian taught that man can arrive at spiritual excellence by the development of his spiritual faculties, through his own choice and the quickening power of the Spirit. Three views on the union of soul and body were advocated: 1. Pre-existence of the soul before union with the body. 2. The soul is transmitted through Adam to all generations. 3. Each soul is created with the body at birth. Each had its advocates. But the third view finally prevailed.

8. Doctrine of the Church. The world's social life is impure. Against this stands the Church—organized purity, God's children, his bride, the foreshadowing of his everlasting kingdom. It is a living body of believers. There may be unbelievers in the body, but, in the main, the Church is pure, and God will take care to preserve its character. The object of the Church is the culture of the soul, until released from its bondage. It is the depository of the divine truth. God has furnished in the Church, according to Cyprian and Irenæus, the universal operation of the Spirit.

9. The Sacraments. There was a disposition, on the part of some teachers, to associate a sacrificial union of the Holy Ghost with the water in baptism. Origen says that baptism is the beginning and the source of the gifts of the Spirit. Baptismal regeneration, though not taught, had, nevertheless, thus early, its supporters. Gregory of Nazianzus called baptism "the sacrament of the new birth;" Cyprian spoke of the "regenerating water," and Augustine of "the sacrament of birth and regeneration." The Greeks were much inclined to emphasize the spiritual gifts, while the Latins were more cautious, and attached great importance to the previous spiritual state of the baptized. In the general faith of the Church there was no belief in baptismal regeneration. The act of baptism, in the adult, was the human sign of a divine act of grace already performed upon the soul. Tertullian disapproved of infant baptism; Origen favored it, and described it as an existing usage; Cyprian, speaking for the Western Church, did the same. The usage was universally acknowledged by the middle of the third century. The Lord's Supper was the human sign, divinely appointed to keep in mind the death of Christ. Ordinary bread, and wine mixed with water, were employed as symbols. After the second century none but baptized persons could partake of the Lord's Supper. During the whole of the patristic period there was not a trace of the doctrine of transubstantiation, save in a theory stated by the fertile Irenæus, that the elements, after consecration, have the effective power of the body and blood of Christ. All the Christian writers, down to the middle of the fourth century, looked upon the elements solely as symbols of the body and blood of Christ. The words, "This is my body," were construed as a liturgical accommodation, meaning the representation of the body and blood by the bread and wine, and in no sense a substantial transformation.

10. Eschatology. The Church loved to think of a peaceful and happy future. The early coming of Christ was expected by many of the laity, while some of the more serious teachers and scholars thought they saw in the New Testament abundant warrant for the early introduction of the millennium. But all such hopes were soon eclipsed in the Christian mind by the broad and white harvest-field to be reaped before his coming. In the Alexandrian theology we find the first traces of a purgatorial fire. Origen made the final fire, which should destroy the world, as the same fire which should purify all souls. During the first three centuries the general Church believed that all who die enter an intermediate state, but after the beginning of the fourth century the opinion prevailed that Hades would be the temporary home of only the wicked, while the righteous would immediately enter into the presence of God. The present life was regarded as the only probationary possibility. The idea of a second probation was of much later origin, and belongs to the superstitions which grew up, most likely, from pagan and Oriental sources. The final restoration of the wicked was advocated by Origen, who even admitted the devil to its benefits. But here, as in other fields, the Church was slow to be guided by the warm fancy and generous sympathy of the Egyptian enthusiast.

11. The Effect of the Nicene Council. The process of theological adjustment was slow, and attended with great difficulty. The differences in race, climate, and intelligence were serious, and, before a theological consensus was arrived at, there was the appearance of hopeless diversity. But the Council of Nicæa had the great effect, not alone of settling the controversy on the divinity of Christ, and placing it beyond doubt as a fundamental doctrine, but of teaching the Church that there was to be a written standard of universal faith, determined by the Church in its representative capacity; that the doctrines of the Church would not be left to the temporary triumph of some acute dialectician; that an emperor could not make and ordain a Christian creed with any hope of success; and that theology is not a stagnant science, which admits of no enlargement with the flight of centuries and with the growth of the general domain of knowledge. It is not likely that, notwithstanding the controversies on theological questions, the faith of the Christians was seriously agitated. The hair-splitting sophistries of Christian debaters, who had brought their pagan dialectics with them into the Christian fold, did not disturb the average Christian. Those men had little to do with the determination of doctrine. The general body of plodding and fervent members, who knew no logic but the facts of the gospels, were the principal agents who kept the Church close to its original moorings. The theology of the matter-of-fact believer was exact and closely knit. He was not disconcerted by the jargon on the *process* of the Logos towards manifestation, or the *procession* of the Holy Ghost also from the Son, or whether only the wicked enter Hades. He knew that Jesus was born in Bethlehem, that the Holy Ghost was the divine Comforter, and that his Lord would not inflict on him a long suspense after martyrdom before permitting him to behold his face.

The Nicene conclusions, far from being the mere fruit of theologians, were the faith of the great commonwealth of believers throughout Christendom. The real master at Nicæa was neither Athanasius nor Constantine, but the humble believer, who might be keeping his flocks beside the Euphrates, or cultivating his patch of lentils in the Thebaid, or singing his psalms beneath his thatched roof on the outskirt of a dark forest of the Germania of Trajan's day.

Chapter XXII.

ECCLESIASTICAL GOVERNMENT AND THE ROMAN PRIMACY.

1. Revolution in Church Government. The early period of the Church was marked by a simple government. The offices and orders were few, derived from the Scriptures, and administered without ostentation and formality. But the enlargement of territory, the multiplication of societies, the dealing with the lapsed and other classes requiring special dealing, and, above all, the bringing of the Church into union with the state, increased the offices to an alarming extent. The political system of Rome entered more and more into the Christian mind as a model for government. The metropolitan centre and the synodal bond were derived directly from the imperial arrangement for the government of provinces. Under Constantine the Church became only the smaller within the larger empire. Simplicity of government continued until about the end of the second century, but after that the tendency was towards a complex polity. For at least three quarters of a century before Constantine the new taste had exhibited itself, but when he converted Christianity into the state religion all obstacles were removed, and offices multiplied.

2. The Minor Clergy. These began with the subdeacons, who assisted the deacons in subordinate services. The acolyths were assistants to the bishops, in many subordinate relations. At the communion service they filled the cup with wine and water, and could administer the elements alone. The lectors, or readers, appear as a clerical order early in the third century. They had charge of the sacred books of the society, read prescribed passages to the congregation, and usually consisted of ministerial candidates. The catechists were only occasionally a special order, their duties being performed by presbyters, deacons, and lectors. When the congregation was very large they were called into exercise, to propose candidates for admission to the Church. The *hermeneutæ*, or interpreters, interpreted the sermon and scriptural selections into the language of the people, when the language was not Greek or Latin. This was the case in the Carthaginian Church, where the language was Punic. Singers or precentors were used in the larger churches, to aid in music. The lowest rank was the *ostiarii*, or doorkeepers, who served as ushers, preserved order, and had charge of the sacred buildings. These offices were in force by the beginning of the third century. During the following century we find the other subordinate officers: the *economos*, or trustee of Church property; the *defensor*, or attorney; the *notarius*, or secretary, who recorded and preserved official records; the *parabolani*, or nurses of the sick; and the *fossores*, or grave-diggers.

3. The Greater Clergy. The chief clerical work devolved upon the deacons and presbyters, whose functions remained the same as at the beginning. When the Roman Clement wrote his Epistle to the Corinthians, A.D. 70, there was no difference between bishop and presbyter. The presbyter was the pastor, with all the sacred ministerial functions. The bishop was, at the beginning, the same. During all the early centuries he was only the presbyter, but with a larger government, embracing a group or territory of separate societies. Originally, the Church or congregation elected the bishop, and invited neighboring bishops to consecrate him to his new office. Then, in the third century, the bishop was elected by brother bishops in adjoining territory, after the manner of the election of an apostle. By the middle of the third century, the election of a bishop was confirmed by the votes of all the bishops of the province, in presence of the laity, and by their consent. The Council of Nicæa gave the bishops of the province the right to elect without lay participation—a mode very popular in the West, but not in the East, where the laity continued to exercise the right of both veto and direct election. The bishops were elected sometimes by acclamation of the multitude, as in the case of Cyprian, and the bishops, presbyters, and other clergy were compelled to submit. It is historically true that, in such cases, the choice was generally a wise one. The people knew their man.

4. Powers of the Bishop. With time the prerogatives of the bishop enlarged. At first his power was limited by dependence on the co-operation of the presbyters. He could nominate the clergy, but could not advance to orders without the vote of the presbyters. He could not determine doctrinal questions, or discipline, or general administration. He had to summon the clergy of the diocese, and submit the questions, and abide by their vote. The government of the local society was vested in the hands of the laity, and the presbyter was only the spiritual guide. The process by which the bishop became the chief officer was this: From the first society another radiated, and still others from them, until there was a group of churches, which extended even into the suburban parts. The parent Church was held in highest esteem. The bishop's residence was supposed to be in connection with it, but over each Church there was a presbyter, and over all the bishop, whose spiritual functions were no greater than those of the humblest presbyter in the diocese. There was some variation, according to place, in the independence of the individual society. In Constantinople, for example, the presbyters of the mother Church served the three filial churches in order. There was a tendency of the richer suburban churches towards independence. In time they were grouped, and had their bishop, who was called a *chorepiscopos*, or rural bishop. This office became a source of serious disorder. The rural bishop was not acknowledged to be equal to his brother in office in the city. Several of the provincial synods of the fourth century took from the rural bishops the right of nominating the clergy. Finally, the *chorepiscopos* was abolished by the council of Laodicea, A.D. 341, and of Sardica, A.D. 347.

5. **The Metropolitan Authority** was closely related to the diocese. The word *metropolitan* does not appear before the Council of Nicæa. But the idea had been in force from the earlier period of the expansion of the Church. The city where the gospel was planted, and from which it extended into other regions of the province, was the maternal city of the Church of the whole territory. In due time other societies, remote from the centre, were formed, which grew in number and importance, and were grouped into dioceses. But the connections were kept up with the central authority. Rome, for example, was the original Italian Church. But other cities in due time received the gospel, such as Tusculum, Tibur, Velitræ, Ostia, and

Portus, each of which became a diocese, with a separate bishop. Now the bishop living in the original society was the metropolitan. He was always regarded with peculiar reverence, because of his supposed attachment to the doctrines and usages of the Church. The metropolitan had important rights. He could convene provincial synods, preside over them, and see that the conclusions were enforced. There were six metropolitans—those of Rome, Antioch, Jerusalem, Alexandria, Ephesus, and Corinth.

6. The Patriarchate. This was a higher office than the metropolitan. The number of metropolitans was reduced to four general patriarchates—Rome, Alexandria, Antioch, and Constantinople. This was an imitation of the political division by Constantine of the whole Roman Empire into four prefectures. The patriarchs consecrated the metropolitans and the bishops of the diocese, summoned the synods of the whole patriarchate, had supervision of all general ecclesiastical affairs, even the court of final appeal, and could have legates at foreign courts. The patriarchate of Alexandria comprised six provinces; Antioch, fifteen; Constantinople, twenty-eight; and Jerusalem, three.

7. The Roman Bishop. Many things contributed to give pre-eminence to the Roman bishop. The Church in Rome was distinguished for its conservatism. It was firm in the midst of many heresies. After the overthrow of Jerusalem it was believed to be the oldest apostolic Church. Its good quality of faith was well known, or, as Paul says, had been "spoken of throughout the whole world." In the giving of alms, in missionary zeal, and in doctrinal purity the Roman Christians had no superiors. The certain residence of Paul in Rome, and the already growing impression of

Peter's sojourn there, were important apostolical associations, which clothed the Roman society with great sanctity. By the middle of the second century there was frequent mention of the primacy of Rome. In the early part of the third century there was a revision of the Recognitions, in which the idea of a Roman primacy was made very prominent. So soon as this intimation was expressed, there were strong views against it. Cyprian declared that each bishop is equal, and that the Church is a unit. "Be it so," cried Origen, when he heard of the new Roman claim to foundation by Peter, and therefore pre-eminence; "but if Peter is the only one on whom the Church is built, what becomes of John and the other apostles? Is Peter, forsooth, the only one against whom the gates of hell should not prevail?" Irenæus spoke in a similar strain. And yet the trend of the general policy was towards Roman centralization. Each new Roman bishop advanced beyond the claims of his predecessor. Zephyrinus held that he alone should be arbiter on the discipline of penitents; Victor assumed the same right on the Easter controversy; and Stephen asserted a similar claim on the baptism of heretics. The resisting force lay in the Eastern Church, where Antioch was leader. But there was little cohesion in the East. It was regarded as provincial, while in spiritual affairs Rome came constantly into more prominent leadership. In due time little or no attention was paid to the Eastern protests. When Firmilian, the obscure bishop of Cappadocian Cæsarea, dared to charge Stephen of Rome with boasting of episcopal superiority, he was only laughed at in the Western metropolis.

8. Constantinople was called New Rome. When Constantine made the obscure Byzantium, which had been subordinate to Heraclea, the capital of Thrace, his vast capital and the centre of imperial authority, much advantage to the Church was expected. But the result was not satisfactory. When he passed away there was little purity left. The palace became a nest of intrigue and revolution. The Turkey of our times, with its plots and counter-plots, and its nameless corruptions, is only the modern reflection of the depravity which dwelt in the imperial home of the successors of Constantine. The members of the court frequently hurled theological terms at each other; while the wrangles of schismatics were transferred to the homes of the nobility, with little loss of bitterness. As in the Bosphorus one sees the tumultuous flow of northern and southern waters, so, beside its beautiful and historic banks, in the fourth century, one could see the meeting of all the conflicting thoughts which agitated the whole Eastern Church. Each new party hoped for success from imperial favor. The agitations around the eastern half of the Mediterranean became so serious as to retard missionary operations, to threaten unity, and to promote spiritual decline. In the West the life was more steady. There was no emperor to lean upon. When an Eastern heresy reached Rome, it was generally throttled, or vivisected, without much ado. The Roman Church life had the equipoise of power, and of faith in its high destiny. It was willing to hear any new thing which came to it, but not to go out in quest of novel ideas. It possessed neither the wish nor the talent for theological invention. It was willing to wait, and to profit by blunders elsewhere, but not to look backward, except to gather up supporting traditions for a steadier and farther march into the future.

Chapter XXIII.

SACRED SEASONS AND PUBLIC WORSHIP.

1. The Weekly Festivals. The festal cycle of the Christian world gradually assumed fixed form. The tendency was towards an enlargement upon the apostolic limitation. But each addition was achieved after heated discussion. The Jewish Christian, after losing the traces of the Jewish calendar, was slow to add any new day which might be suggested by the Gentile Christian. The first day of the week came constantly into more frequent use than the seventh for sacred services. But the Jewish Christians continued to use both the first and seventh days, until the first generation had disappeared, when the influence of Gentile Christianity became predominant. Barnabas, Ignatius, and Justin furnish positive proof of the early substitution of the first for the seventh day. That it was called Sunday because of a Saxon god, is an old error, for which there is no foundation. It was a day of gladness, because of the great gift of our Lord's resurrection, the day of new light, the day of the sun (ἡ ἡλιου ἡμερα). Wednesday and Friday were also used as days of service, but never in the high sense of the Sunday service. The Wednesday service was designed to commemorate our Lord's arrest by the Jewish council, and Friday to commemorate his death. Those days, the fourth and sixth of the week, were called the *stations* —a military term, as a reminder that the Christian is a soldier, and must be on his guard against the enemies of Christ.*

2. The Yearly Festivals. The Passover was the most important. It signified the festal commemoration of the sparing of the first-born in Egypt, and, in a Christian sense, the memorial celebration of the death of Christ. The great Easter controversy arose on the duration of the Easter fast. It was only a question of a few hours, but the whole Church was divided on the trivial matter. The Western Christians contending for the longer time, and the Eastern for the shorter. From Gaul to Pontus the discussion swept. Synods were called, and the strife became bitter. But the Western view prevailed, and those who held to the Eastern opinion either withdrew their opposition or concentrated into a little sect, the Quartodecimanians, whose home was confined to Asia Minor and proconsular Africa. They had but a short existence. The Roman bishop Victor refused to acknowledge as Christians all who sympathized with the Eastern view, and excommunicated them. Pentecost gained additional strength in the Christian mind. While the Jew celebrated it in thankful commemoration of the harvest, and the gift of the Law on Sinai, the Christian revered it, and placed it very high in his calendar, in commemoration of the outpouring of the Spirit after our Lord's ascension. Epiphany became a holyday in the latter half of the fourth century. The first definite trace of it is A.D. 360. The Christmas celebration does not seem to have been thought of as yet, either in the Eastern or Western Church.

3. Martyr Days. The growing reverence for the

* Tertullian says: "Statio de militari nomen accepit, nam et militaria dei sumus."—"De Orat." cap. 19.

martyrs led to special services on the anniversary of their death. By a happy thought, the day of the martyr's death was called his "birthday." Processions were made on these days to the scene of the martyrdom, churches were erected over the remains of the martyrs, memorial sermons were preached on the anniversary, and the special day was added to the calendar. This tendency, innocent and natural in the first four centuries, afterwards became a superstition, and brought many evils into the Church. On the memorial martyr days the Lord's Supper was celebrated, with a view to continued fellowship with them. It was called an oblation or sacrifice for martyrs—*sacrificium pro martyribus.* It must be remembered, however, that during the entire patristic period these memorial days for martyrs were no part of the order of the Church. They grew out of the fame and merit of Christians, who died sooner than renounce their faith in Christ. The martyrology of the Roman Catholic Church, the large use of images, and the realistic services, were all of much later and less spiritual origin.

4. Churches. The church was on the plan of the Jewish temple and the synagogue. It was called the Lord's house, the house of prayer, the house of the Church. The architecture of the first churches was simple, and gave no promise of the subsequent splendor of the basilica and the cathedral. The interior of the church consisted of three parts—the vestibule, the nave, and the choir. The congregation assembled in the nave, and here the pulpit was erected, the Scriptures read, and the sermon delivered. The choir was used alone for the clergy; it corresponded to the holy of holies of the Jewish temple. It was separated from the nave by a lattice or railing, and curtains, and was elevated above the nave. In the centre of the choir was the wooden table bearing the symbols of our Lord's death. In the rear, following the semicircular wall, the clergy sat, while the bishop sat on a cathedra, or raised seat.

5. Images. There was, very early, a distaste for all representations of deity or sacred characters. Clement of Alexandria expressed the sentiment of his age: "The custom of daily looking on the representation of the Divine Being desecrates his dignity." The time had not, as yet, arrived when Christian art was employed to clothe our Lord's person with ethereal beauty and sweetness. The theology of the times attributed to him the sad and homely visage of prophecy,* and it is a quaint fancy of Tertullian that he could never have been despised of men, and have suffered death for them, if in his person he had manifested his heavenly glory. Origen held that his whole person was repulsive. The Eastern Church has never deviated from this view. In the Græco-Russian Church of to-day, whether amid the barbaric splendor of the Cathedral of St. Isaac, in St. Petersburg, or in the more ancient Church of the Transfiguration on the Kremlin, it is the same sad and austere countenance which we discover in the ancient frescoes of Ravenna. The Council of Elvira, A.D. 305, declared against the use of all images in sacred buildings. The Western Church was inclined, early, to the use of images, and this preference was one of the causes which finally led to the division of the East and the West.

---

* Isa. liii. 2, 3. Cf. Tertullian, "Adv. Judæos," cap. 14.

Chapter XXIV.

ECCLESIASTICAL DISCIPLINE.

1. Careful Training was early observed in the spiritual life of the Church. No sooner was a society organized than the closest attention was paid to the religious instruction of the young. The converts of Pentecost were immediately received into the fellowship of believers. But the work was only just begun. There must be edification. Each believer was regarded as a temple, not finished, but susceptible of all beautiful and symmetrical forms. He must be built up. Hence, full provision was made for instruction and training. Paul's epistles abound in intimations that constant attention was paid to the domestic training for Christian life, and for careful instruction in Biblical knowledge. The new adult convert had everything to learn. He had just come in from paganism. No miracle could compensate for the previous absence of religious truth. When one embraced the new faith, or, as the phrase of the time went, "laid off the toga for the pallium," he was a blank.

2. The Catechumens were required to pass through a severe discipline. There was no fixed time for terminating the catechumenate. While the apostles baptized immediately on profession of faith, the patristic Church moved more slowly, for experience taught them that nothing was lost by a longer process before full membership. There were three classes of catechumens — the hearers, the kneelers, and the petitioners. The hearers could come to the general service, and hear the sermon and the lessons, but could not remain for prayers. The kneelers could hear also the prayers, and even the prayer of the imposition of hands. The petitioners could hear the entire service, and petition for baptism at the next public appointing, which was usually Easter Sunday. When the petition was accepted the names of the candidate and his sponsors were recorded in the diptych, or register. Then came a close examination, or "scrutiny," which lasted twenty days. When public baptism and reception took place the new member was admitted to the Eucharist. After the period of persecution had closed, the time for the duration of the catechumenate became briefer than before. The Apostolical Constitutions favored three years. The Synod of Elvira laid down two. But the Synod of Agde shortened the time to eight months.

3. The Apostates were the more difficult class to manage. The temptations to apostasy were numerous. In some regions the process of restoration continued for years. In others, when penitents were ready to suffer martyrdom, the ordeal was brief. In the African Church many apostates secured letters of peace from men just before suffering martyrdom, and with these as authority they boldly demanded admission again into the Church. One man, Lucian, boldly declared that he had granted peace to all apostates in North Africa, and had declared their sins absolved; and Cyprian, in a gentle mood, cried aloud that the Church must keep peace with its martyrs. There were two classes of sins—the venial and the mortal. But martyrdom was regarded as the completion of any penitential experience. In the latter part of the third century the penitents were more largely classified: mourners, hearers, kneelers, and bystanders. A bystander was the most advanced. He could advance up the nave of the church, join in all the prayers of the Church, and witness the celebration of the Lord's Supper, but not participate in it. During all the stages towards restoration the penitent must give practical proof of sincerity by abstaining from all diversions, by observing all the public fasts, by giving liberally towards the support of the poor, and by assisting in burying the dead. Restoration was completed by admitting the penitent to the Lord's Supper, by the prayer of absolution and reconciliation, and by the imposition of hands by the bishop.

4. The Penitential Presbyter was the special officer who supervised the penitents during all the stages of restoration. It was his duty to see that all requirements were met, that the bishop was duly notified of the progress made by the penitent, and that the time was fixed for final restoration. This early office in the Church has been wrongly supposed to be a warrant for the modern confessional. But the penitential presbyter was in no sense a confessor. His duty was to hear, guard, and advise, but never to receive private confession. He was the representative of the Church to impart, and not to receive. This office was abolished A.D. 390, and was never restored until many centuries afterwards, by the institution of the confessional.

Chapter XXV.

CHRISTIAN LIFE AND USAGES.

1. **The Charitable Spirit** of the Church in the apostolic time took larger form in the patristic period. There was no need of Christians in one place which did not awaken sympathy everywhere. When Cyprian saw that the Numidian Christians could not pay the required ransom of their captive brethren, he took a large collection in Carthage for that purpose, and sent it to them, with a letter full of fraternal expressions. Dionysius of Corinth lauded the Roman society as the helper of Christians, without distinction, from its very origin. Dionysius of Alexandria, in a letter to Stephen, Bishop of Rome, pays the same tribute. Basil of Cappadocia wrote a letter of thanks to Rome for money sent to him to redeem captive Christians from their barbarous foes. Demetrius drew a striking picture of the sacrifice of Christians during the pestilence in Alexandria. Gifts for the support of the Church were made at each service; often these consisted in wares, or produce of the soil, according to the pursuits of the people. In the East a fixed sum, or the tithes, was held to be the proper standard of annual beneficence. But in the West there was no rule. The great teachers opposed any defined measure, saying that the Lord required all that could be spared. A careful record, the *matricula*, was preserved of all the details of the benefactions.

2. The Incentives to Knowledge were very great. The transition from paganism to Christianity was a thorough revolution. The field of Christian knowledge was a new world. In the schools catechetical exercises prevailed. The secular sciences were subordinated to religion. Christianity had not built up its great libraries, but the books written by the leading Christian thinkers were already read with profound interest. Each Church was the centre of knowledge. Copies of the Scriptures were expensive, but were multiplied, and each Church possessed several copies, together with expository and other works. All these were for the benefit of the congregation in the intervals of service and during the week. There was a special room for the use of books, which was called the *Phrontisterion*, or thinking-shop. One of the first impulses of the new Christian who was possessed of means was to employ copyists, and have the entire Scriptures transcribed, for loaning or presenting to either churches or private circles. Even during the time of persecution so many copies of the Scriptures had found their way into private hands that the pagan wrath was aroused. During the Diocletian persecution, especially, their possessors were ordered to deliver up vast numbers of them. Even the pagan enemies secured copies, for the works of Celsus, Porphyry, Hierocles, and others give abundant proof that the authors must have had a personal inspection of some portions of the Bible.

3. The Domestic Life was in direct contrast with everything pagan. There were, therefore, no reminders of the old idolatry. The typical Greek and Roman houses had been profusely adorned with figures, busts, and monograms of favorite divinities. But even this was a decline from the early Roman austerity. For nearly two centuries after the founding of Rome no citizen had so far accommodated himself to the superstition of Greece or Egypt as to erect a statue to any deity. But the times brought sad changes. The excavations in Pompeii, and the many memorials of art from the Roman ruins, show how thoroughly the later art was superseded by a gross idolatry. The Christian's first impulse was to put away all such things. He lost no time in blotting out every trace of the obedient Mercury, the majestic Apollo, the generous Ceres, and even the omnipotent Jove, from doorway, court, and hall. But he was not satisfied with this severe absence of all symbolism. Even the more cautious Christian writers encouraged a safe and proper counterpart to the polytheistic symbolism of their pagan adversaries. Clement of Alexandria urged the use of Christian symbols on seal rings, and named, as proper figures, the dove, as an image of the Holy Ghost; the fish, with reference to the call of Zebedee's sons to be fishers of men; the ship, as an emblem of the advancing Church; the lyre, as the type of Christian joy; and the anchor, as an expression of hope. The crucifix was never used.

4. Epistolary Writings. Every great teacher was an industrious correspondent. Paul had set the example, and it was diligently followed by his successors in evangelization. Epistolary writing had long been a favorite Roman fashion. Cicero, Seneca, Pliny, and many other authors chose the form of the letter to an individual, in order to inform the public of their views on many special subjects. The fathers in the Church chose, therefore, a means of information which they found in use already, both from apostolic and pagan example. The letters of Polycarp and Origen, and the eighty-six warm and nervous epistles of Cyprian, are only a small part of the epistolary inheritance of those times to the later Church. A number of the apologists addressed their works to Roman emperors. The Christians were largely represented among the commercial and laboring classes, and often changed their abodes. They followed the lines of commerce. As in the United States the Christian people from the Atlantic seaboard have gone into the far western regions, and taken with them their Christian spirit, and built churches, so, in the third and fourth centuries, the Christians observed the new openings of business and planted Christian societies in the places where they settled. Between the old and new societies a frequent correspondence was maintained. Christians who went upon a journey, for any purpose, were often the bearers of letters, to be delivered on the way or on reaching the place of destination. When these letters arrived, being on a durable fabric, either papyrus or parchment, they became the permanent possessions of the society or the individual receiving them. The synodical letters, which were written after each session of the provincial synod to similar bodies in other provinces, will convey some idea of the extent to which official relationship was carried. When action was taken on a schism, or on any special subject, the utmost promptness was employed to communicate the fact far and wide, while a bishop, on being chosen to the office, was equally prompt in sending notification of his election to his colleagues in any part of Christendom.

5. The Travels of the Fathers. The most distant parts of the Church were brought into close relationship, also, by personal visitation. The fathers were busy travellers. Many parts of the East were even safer then for the stranger than they are to-day. The Greek and Roman authors were in the habit of visiting places which they described. Homer certainly saw the Troad, for the Iliad bears internal evidence of a personal examination. Herodotus journeyed in many lands, now among the priests of the Upper Nile, and now in Asia Minor, endeavoring to verify the country by contact with the people and their land. Sallust visited Africa, in order to be faithful in his picture of Jugurtha. Jerome lingered long in Palestine, in order to make sure work in his exegetical studies. Papias, Bishop of Hieropolis, conceived the happy thought of visiting Palestine, and trying to find among the most aged people of different countries some who had seen our Lord in the flesh, "for," said he, "I did not think that I could get so much aid from the books as from the words of those living and remaining." Out of this tour grew his Explanation of the Discourses of our Lord.

Polycarp, in his extreme age, or about A.D. 158, visited Rome, to come to an understanding with the bishop Anicetus, concerning the baptism of heretics and the observance of Easter. Irenæus labored in Asia Minor, Gaul, and Rome. From the journey of Hegesippus to Alexandria came one of the richest points of Christian research, the finding of Manetho's catalogue of the kings of Egypt. In these days we regard the journey to Ararat as an undertaking of remarkable difficulty, but Julius made it, in the interest of sacred science, and identified it as the mountain on which the ark had rested. He also visited the Dead Sea, and located the site of Sodom and Gomorrah. Clement of Alexandria was a diligent traveller over three continents. Origen appears to have visited every part of the Christian world, including far-off Persia. Rufinus studied the monastic life, by personal observation among the monks of the Nitrian desert. Hieronymus was an ideal traveller in the interest of sacred learning. He located himself in Palestine, in order to learn the idiomatic construction of the Biblical text from contact with the people. He employed, as a special teacher in Hebrew, a Jew, who instructed him by night, lest the Christians might learn of it, and take offence. He even visited Cilicia, in order to learn the deep force and subtle meaning of Paul's epistles. It need not occasion surprise that, with such pains, Hieronymus should easily stand at the head of the Latin Church, and that to his patient and thorough scholarship the world should be indebted for the Vulgate version. This is the beautiful justification which he gave for his sojourn in Palestine:

"As the history of the Greeks is better understood by him who has seen Athens, and Virgil's third book by him who has sailed from the Troad to Sicily, and from there to the mouth of the Tiber, so do the Holy Scriptures become clearer to him who has seen Judæa with his own eyes, and has made himself acquainted with the recollections of the old cities and the name of the places, whether they are the same or have been changed. Therefore I had it in heart to undertake this work, in connection with the most learned Jews, so that I have wandered through the country from which all the churches of Christ take their tone."

Chapter XXVI.

THE CHURCH IN THE CATACOMBS.

1. The Roman Catacombs are excavations, often at great depth, made by the Christians for the burial of the dead. The Roman never continued his warfare with other faiths after death. He allowed the Christians every liberty in the disposition of their dead. The catacombs had been already in use by the Jewish residents of Rome. At first they probably made a mere opening in the hillside, or a hollow beneath a shelving wall, as their fathers had done in Palestine from remote times. But, later, the Jewish burial-place became an approach to the Christian catacomb. Some of these Jewish wall catacombs are still in existence; as, for example, one opposite the catacomb of San Sebastiano, and another nearer Rome, in the Randaniani vineyard. The galleries are the same as those of the Christian catacombs, only less ornate and regular. The Jewish type is everywhere recorded by the seven-branched candlestick or other Hebrew symbols.

2. Roman Burial and Cremation. In the earlier Roman times, burial was the method in use. But cremation came into use later, probably as a result of the importation of the Persian idea of the evil in matter. But burial was still preferred by many of the older Roman families, as can be seen in the monument of the Scipios, before the Porta Capena, of Rome, now within the walls. The graves of the Nasos, four Italian miles from Rome, on the Via Flaminia, consist of chambers hewn in the tufa, with horizontal niches for the bodies, in precisely the same way as the Christian catacomb. There was one difference, however, between the pagan and the Christian burial-place. The pagan catacomb was exclusive, like the palace, being confined to the family. But the Christian catacomb was for the whole brotherhood of faith. The ties of life were to continue after death. The poor and rich should be together in death, as they had worshipped and suffered side by side in life. No private burial-place in Rome could be alienated by sale. In all deeds the burial-place was exempted in the sale of a villa and grounds.

3. The Discovery of the Christian Catacomb. The modern discovery of the Roman catacomb took place in May, 1578. Some workmen in a field along the Via Salaria came across a mysterious opening in the earth, which led to the finding of passages, frescoes of infinite variety, Greek and Latin inscriptions, and several sarcophagi. From that hour subterranean Rome took its place as a priceless storehouse of Christian science. Until then the burial-places of the early Christians had awakened no interest and possessed no meaning. They had been, practically, unknown since the early Church. Hieronymus relates that, when a schoolboy in Rome, he and some of his companions frequently went down into the graves and looked at the dust of the martyrs, and that they wandered through the long passages and caverns, and saw the bodies on either side, and that the darkness was so profound that his boyish imagination was strongly excited by the scene, so that he could not help thinking of the words of David, "Let them go down quick into hell," and of the words of Vergil, "Terror surrounds me; even the silence itself is horrible."

4. Bosio and the Study of the Catacombs. Antonio Bosio, born in 1575, was the first to reveal the rich treasures which had lain concealed for thirteen centuries. No difficulty was too great for his tireless spirit. One catacomb after another was opened by him. He created a new science. He devoted thirty years to these explorations and to the preparation of his great work, "Roma Soterranea," and died in 1629. His book did not appear until after his death. John Evelyn, who visited Rome in 1645, and Bishop Burnet, who made a sojourn there forty years later, were the first writers to reveal to the English world the extent and significance of the Christian catacombs. During the time which has since elapsed the catacombs have been emptied of their greatest treasures, which have been deposited in the museum of St. John Lateran, the Vatican, and other places in Rome. Some have drifted into other parts of Europe. The Christian Museum of the Berlin University contains the best collection of memorials from the catacombs to be found outside of Rome. These, with other objects illustrating Christian history, have been gathered through the energy and zeal of Professor Piper.

5. De Rossi. The descent into a catacomb is through a church or chapel, which has been built over the entrance. The passages vary in size and length. The aggregate extent is a matter of conjecture. De Rossi, the greatest of all the later explorers and writers in this rich department, supposes the length of the passages of all the catacombs to be equal to the length of the entire Italian peninsula. Marchi reaches an estimate of a third larger. It is not likely that all the catacombs have been explored. As late as 1848 the magnificent catacomb of Prætextatus was discovered,

ROMAN CATACOMBS.

while in 1874 De Rossi discovered the catacomb of St. Petronilla, a small but very rich storehouse of sepulchral Christian art. No approach to the probable number of fixed paintings, carvings, and inscriptions which have been taken from the catacombs can be made with safety. In the Lateran Museum, in the sarcophagi alone, there are two hundred and seventy-six scriptural carvings.

6. Familiarity with the Scriptures. The catacombs were continued as places of burial down to about A.D. 410, when the West Goths plundered Rome. They tell the story of the faith and usages, and especially of the Scriptures, down to that date. Every part of the Old Testament was known to the Christians. The word-pictures of the Old Testament are everywhere reproduced in rude frescoes. Noah in the ark, the offering of Isaac, Moses taking off his shoes, the translation of Elijah, Daniel in the lions' den, and the three Hebrews in the fiery furnace were favorite topics, as bearing on the tribulations of the Church of the time. The New Testament furnished many themes. No scene in our Lord's ministry remained unnoticed. Such subjects as indicated a brighter future, as the ever-growing vine, and the sower and the seed, were special favorites with the rude Christian artist of the earliest period. Many Scriptural citations were employed. The scroll, standing out of a cistus, or manuscript-case, was frequent. Paul was represented in this way, with evident reference to his writings. Where two scrolls lay before a figure, the meaning was that the deceased made no difference between the Old and the New Testament, but accepted both as the equal and inspired word of God.

7. Orthodoxy and Christian Defence are plainly taught in the symbolism of the catacombs. Christ was everywhere mentioned, either by name or rude figure. The humblest grave bore at least the fish, which, in Greek, constituted the monogram of Christ; ΙΧΘΥΣ (Iesus Christos, Theou Uios, Soter—Jesus Christ, Son of God, Saviour). But no word or picture has been found in these silent passages which calls up any of the violent controversies which swept over the Church. Neither has there been found a suggestion of an heretical vagary. Sometimes pagan pictures were given, but always to teach with greater force the Messiah's kingdom. Three representations of Christ as Orpheus have been found, two by Bosio, in the catacomb of Domatilla, and one by De Rossi, in that of St. Callista. In the two former he sits between two trees, crowned with the Phrygian cap, and playing on a lyre. Beasts come thronging about him, and hear his notes, and are charmed and tamed by the melody. Doves, peafowl, horses, sheep, serpents, tortoises, a dog, and a hare at a lion's feet, hear the music, and mingle together in Edenic simplicity and peace. The whole is a symbol of our Lord's peaceful empire, and also an indication of the disposition of early Christians at Rome, as in the theology of Alexandria, to make paganism bring its offering to our Lord's altar. Theseus slaying the Minotaur was made a type of David slaying Goliath. One beautiful figure, gilt on glass, and dating from the end of the fourth century, represents our Lord with radiated head. He holds the globe of universal sovereignty in his hand, while at his feet stands the cistus, containing the gospel scroll. The Trinity was always represented in such a way as to indicate an equality of persons. De Rossi furnishes examples of firm faith in this doctrine, where the monogram of Christ is combined with the triangle.

8. **The Representations of Christ** were all of the cheerful, hopeful, and triumphant type. Only twice, among the sculptures of the Lateran Museum, is he represented during his Passion. He everywhere appears as the Good Shepherd. The catacombs received the bodies of martyrs in many a bitter persecution, but the relatives and friends of the departed uttered no syllable of sorrow. The word *death* is always avoided. "*In Pace*" was the universal legend. Rest and triumph were uppermost in the mind. The dead were, at last, at peace. The grave was surrounded with images of beauty, peace, and joy. It was only after the persecutions were over, and the authors had taken their place in oblivion, that any symbol of suffering was placed in a Roman catacomb. The record of martyrdom was studiously avoided, not only that the Christian might give no indication of disputing the "divine pre-emi-

nence of the Man of Sorrows," but that the Christian was not willing to show, even by figures on the wall of a tomb, that he remembered the agony which a persecuting hand had produced. Death had no terror to him, and the persecutor only hastened the day of peace. From the symbolism in the catacomb one would think that the Christians were living in palaces, and that kings were their servants. The hare, feeding on grapes, the luxuriant palm-tree, the vase of flowers, the loaf of bread, and the dove with the olive-branch, are met with on tablets taken from all the catacombs.

9. **The Historical Suggestions** are sometimes very rich. An epitaph in the cemetery of St. Domatilla, dating from the first century, shows the early entrance of Christianity into the imperial household. The clank of the slave's chain was never heard in a Christian home. So completely and promptly did slavery disappear that of the eleven thousand epigraphs from the catacombs, only six, and two of these doubtful, contain any allusion to the evil, and then only in brief and simple language. There is not a trace of Mariolatry in any early inscription or symbol of a catacomb. The word Maria never occurs until A.D. 381, and then only after the word Livia. The earlier inscriptions were brief, like the breathings of the stricken soul, such as, "To the dearest mother," "To the sweetest child," "God raise thy soul," or "Peace to thy spirit." Later, however, when the catacomb was used only as a cemetery, and not also as a place of refuge from the destroyer, the epigraphs were more fulsome and rhetorical. A beautiful epigraph, "Received to God," dating from A.D. 217, but frequently repeated afterwards, proves that the poor soul had passed through its ordeal here, and needed no purgatory. In De Rossi's compilation,

comprising 1374 different epigraphs, there is no example of prayer for the dead. Clerical celibacy finds no support in the catacombs or any early tombs. An inscription, found on the Ostian Way, to the wife of a deacon, or sub-deacon, ran thus:

> "Levitæ conjunx Petronia forma pudoris
> His mea deponens sedibus ossa loco.
> Pascite vos lacrimis dulces cum conjuge natæ."

The word "puer" occurred frequently in connection with mature men. It was an index of the association of perpetual youth with the life of the blessed. Hence the surviving daughter or widow or son could well call the deceased father or husband "boy," in view of the immortal youth on which he had now entered. The old Hebrew names had passed away, and the epitaphs show a transition, as in the Puritan depression in England, and in New England history, where a firm faith in God, and a recognition of his special deliverances in sore need, blossomed out beautifully in the names which rejoicing parents gave their children. Hence, in the epigraphs of the catacombs we find such names as the following: Diodorus (God's gift); Fructuosus (Fruit-bringing); Renovatus (Renewed); Anastasia (Risen); Irene (Peace); Sabbatia (Holy-day); and Concordia (Harmony). But all words in the catacombs abounded in hope and joy.

Chapter XXVII.

MONASTICISM.

1. Early Monasticism. Traces of monasticism can be found in all the great Oriental lands. Long before Christianity, and even before the conquests of Alexander in India, the monastic idea had gained great strength. Buddhism and Brahminism made large use of it for extending their doctrines and holding their adherents. The idea of the inherent evil of matter lay at the basis of the monastic principle. It was supposed that contact with society diverted the mind from religious contemplation, and made it less worthy to be the abode of the worshipful spirit. Hence the only safety was to get far from men and their deeds. Nature must be found in her simplicity. The rude elements must be made familiar. These were the thoughts which lay at the bottom of that Christian monasticism which played an important part in the early Church, and extended down to the Reformation, and still holds undisputed sway in the Roman Catholic Church.

2. The Christian Use of Monasticism. Christianity found monasticism already prevalent in the Nazarites of Palestine and the Therapeutæ of Egypt, and it is not strange that, in an age of great social corruption, which overspread all pagan territory, many Christians should see in the separate life a relief from danger.

Persecution favored the tendency towards monasticism. Exile was only another name for a secluded life. Many Christians went voluntarily into remote regions; dwelt in caves or groves; spent the day in works of charity, and much of the night in vigils; and courted nature in her wildest moods. The first monastic stage was voluntary solitude, without any movement towards a separate order. It was the individual mind, looking for spiritual relief, but with no purpose to introduce a new departure in ecclesiastical practice. The next stage was a habit of removal to certain regions, where the monks lived within reach of each other. The third stage was the sanction and regular organization of orders, which took full shape in the Benedictines and similar fraternities. The monks took three vows upon themselves: perpetual fidelity to the life and order; obedience to the abbot, or head of the monastery; and chastity and poverty. A number of the fathers and writers led a monastic life, but without advocacy of a separate order. The tendency grew with the times. The Old Testament was searched for support. Elijah and kindred spirits in Jewish history, and John the Baptist, were brought in to support the monastic taste. Egypt became a favorite place for the monks. Rufinus declared that there were nearly as many monks in the deserts as people in the cities. Montalembert says: "It was a kind of emigration of towns to the desert, of civilization to simplicity, of noise to silence, of corruption to innocence. The current once begun, floods of men, women, and children threw themselves into it, and flowed thither during a century with irresistible force."

3. Notable Examples. Paul of Thebes, in Upper Egypt, was the first Christian hermit. He lived during the persecution under Decius. He is said to have withdrawn to a distant Egyptian cave when twenty-two years of age, and to have lived there until A.D. 340. Anthony, who followed in Paul's footsteps, lived for a long time in extreme poverty in the Egyptian desert. The fame of the life of these two men went into distant lands, and their self-denial was imitated by many people in the countries lying around the eastern end of the Mediterranean. The Pillar Saints constituted a separate class. St. Simeon was the founder of the group. He stood upon the top of a pillar, and spent his life between leaning on a frail railing and standing erect. The height of the pillar was increased as he advanced in virtue. Tennyson puts in his mouth the following confession, after he had spent many years in this life of torture:

"O Lord, Lord,
Thou knowest I bore this better at the first,
For I was strong and hale of body then;
And though my teeth, which now are dropped away,
Would chatter with the cold, and all my beard
Was tagged with icy fringes in the moon,
I drowned the whoopings of the owl with sound
Of pious hymns and psalms, and sometimes saw
An angel stand and watch me, as I sang.
Now am I feeble grown; my end draws nigh—
I hope my end draws nigh: half deaf I am,
So that I scarce can hear the people hum
About the column's base; and almost blind,
And scarce can recognize the fields I know.
And both my thighs are rotted with the dew,
Yet cease I not to clamor and to cry,
While my stiff spine can hold my weary head,
Till all my limbs drop piecemeal from the stone:
Have mercy, mercy; take away my sin!"

CHAPTER XXVIII.

THE AGE OF GREGORY THE GREAT.

1. Growth of the Roman Episcopate.. The march of the Roman bishop towards priority throughout the Christian world was steady. The divisions of the Eastern Empire, the decline of moral life, the universal spread of controversy, and, particularly, the pre-eminent ability of several of the bishops of Rome, were calculated to advance the claims of that patriarchate above all others. The bishop Leo I. was a man of strong intellect, and he did much to clothe himself with power and prestige. But the most eminent incumbent of the Roman episcopate was Gregory, who was called the Great, and ruled A.D. 590–604. Under him every department of the priesthood and the episcopacy advanced in strength. His claims, artfully disguised, were of the most lofty kind.

2. Gregory's Character was of striking quality. He was versatile, and strong in everything he touched. In the development of the hierarchical idea, in theology, liturgical literature, pastoral oversight, monasticism, and missions, he was a master. His hand was felt in the whole field of the ecclesiastical life of his day. Born at Rome (A.D. 540) and descended from an ancient patrician family, he had all the advantages which wealth and education could bring. His parents designed him for service in the state. But he turned his attention to the Church, and advanced rapidly. Yet he showed no disposition to hasten matters. He possessed the virtue of patience in a high degree. Gregory, after his father's death, founded six cloisters, and occupied one himself. He dedicated himself to a life of self-denial. He became deacon of the bishop Pelagius, and was sent as his representative to the court of Constantinople. He wrote a commentary on the Book of Job, and pursued his studies with great energy. On his return to Rome, and the death of the bishop Pelagius, he was chosen to succeed him. He declined the office at first, but afterwards accepted it, but apparently by pressure. Towards the emperor he manifested the profoundest respect, probably with a view to gaining by yielding. He called himself "*servus servorum Dei*"—"servant of the Lord's servants." He devoted himself to the purification of the life of the Church and the enforcement of monastic discipline. He was especially active in his encouragement of missions. He organized the Anglo-Saxon and other missions, and sought to send the gospel into every part of Europe. Under him the authority of the Roman bishop advanced far beyond its former dimensions. He created the papacy of history. He preserved amicable relations with the emperor, though all the while holding firmly his ecclesiastical independence.

Chapter XXIX.

THE EXPANSION OF CHRISTIANITY.

1. The Evangelization of the Nations continued with unabated zeal. Whether in persecution, or after the liberty given by Constantine, the work of missions was carried on with equal fervor. There were three such fields: 1. The poor within the central regions of the empire; 2. The population of such farther provinces as were a firm part of the dominions; and, 3. Those more remote tribes which were hostile to Rome, and were awaiting a good opportunity to satisfy their hunger for conquest by feasting on the dying empire. The Church extended its boundaries by exile, and all the other means employed to destroy it. Both in Rome and in the larger provincial towns, the conflict between the gospel and pagan literature was intense and uninterrupted. The doctrines of Jesus gained steadily on the most finished products of pagan thought. Wordsworth's description of the conquest of the missionary over the Druids of Britain applies equally well to the whole battle-field of three continents:

> "Haughty the Bard—can these weak doctrines blight
> His transports? wither his heroic strain?
> But all shall be fulfilled. The Julian spear
> A way first opened; and, with Roman chains,
> The tidings come of Jesus crucified;
> They came—they spread—the weak, the suffering, hear;
> Receive the faith and in the hope abide."

When Athanasius was banished from Alexandria to northern Gaul, not only did the young society in the latter country enjoy the presence of an heroic example, but the exile himself began his organizing work, and established the diocese of Treves, at that time the capital of Gaul. The general expansion went on rapidly everywhere. Indeed, during the period of suffering the only safety to the Christians lay in their distance from the persecuting centres. Tertullian said defiantly to the whole Roman world: "We are of yesterday, yet we have filled your empire, your cities, your islands, your castles, your towns, your assemblies, your very camps, your tribes, your companies, your palaces, your senate. Your forum and your temples alone are left you!"

2. Eastward. Antioch was the centre from which the light of the gospel radiated eastward into the distant parts of Asia, and westward through Asia Minor. The pathway reached from the shore of the Ægean Sea to the west of China—a longer line of march than Alexander had made. Jerusalem lost its hold as a centre of ecclesiastical power, and its spiritual dominion was divided between Antioch, in the north, and Alexandria, in the south. Cappadocia, and the entire coast of the Euxine Sea east of the Dardanelles and the Bosphorus, were early a mission field. Colchis, Iberia, and Georgia were overspread with missionary laborers. Leontius, bishop of Cæsarea, in Cappadocia, was consecrated bishop of Armenia A.D. 302, with the rank of patriarch. The Bible was translated into Armenian, and a large Christian literature was created. In the third century Persia had so far become evangelized that Ctesiphon became the seat of a flourishing society, and a point of departure for the expansion of Christianity farther east. The doctrines of Zoroaster were attacked by a converted magian, Mobed, who, in a special work, held up to his countrymen the excellence of Christianity. He suffered martyrdom, A.D. 300, but was followed by laborers of equal ardor. Edessa, in Persia, became an important centre of Christian learning. The Nestorian Christians, who were compelled to leave the Roman Empire, took refuge here, and laid the foundations of a rich and influential Syrian literature. Missionary operations were carried on along all the lines of Eastern travel. From the valley of the Tigris and Euphrates the indications are strong that missionaries went far into the interior of India.

3. Africa. The Church in Africa developed with amazing rapidity. Alexandria was the literary centre for the evangelization of the entire delta of the Nile. Missions were planted along either bank, and soon extended far up towards the first cataract, at Philæ, and to the oases on either side of the river. Carthage, the ancient Punic capital, was intimately connected with western Christendom. Many Christians came to both these cities, but in larger numbers to Alexandria, from distant regions, where they became acquainted with the theology and life of the Church, and bore back again the fruits of their study and observation. The whole of proconsular Africa, including Getulia, Mauritania, and Numidia, whose western bounds were washed by the waves of the Atlantic, was evangelized by Roman and Carthaginian Christians. The great number of bishops in the third century dependent on the patriarchate of Carthage furnishes strong evidence of the extent to which Christianity had been propagated in the whole of Western Africa, and of its strong hold upon the people. At the Synod of Labes, near Carthage, A.D. 240 or 242, ninety bishops were present, while two hundred and seventy bishops signed the conclusions of the Council of Carthage, A.D. 308. Abyssinia was converted through two young men, Frumentius and Nedesius, who alone survived the massacre of the members of a scientific expedition conducted by Meropius, a Syrian philosopher. About the end of the fourth century a translation of the Bible was made from the received Greek Testament of the Alexandrian Church into the old language of Abyssinia. The Abyssinian Church has always remained in connection with Alexandria, its boast being: "We drink from the fountain of the patriarch of Alexandria." Feeble as Abyssinian Christianity is, it has preserved its existence, through an unbroken succession of Christian governors, from the fourth century to the nineteenth. With all its error, it may in truth be called the Waldensian Church of the Switzerland of Africa.

4. **The Balkan Peninsula.** The central field of interest was the continent of Europe. Christian missionaries continued the labors of Paul, and carried the gospel through Mœsia to the Danube. Macedonia had numerous Christian societies, while even Illyricum had two dioceses. By A.D. 310 three bishops lived in Philippopolis, in Thrace. The contact of the Goths north of the Danube, in Dacia, with Christianity, was a most important event. It was the opening of a new field of evangelistic labor, and had the important effect of bringing the gospel into relation with the many Teutonic tribes which constituted the eastern Germany of those times. A Gothic bishop, Theophilus, was a member of the Nicene Council. It was, however, through the labors of Ulfilas, a Gothic convert to Christianity, that the gospel spread widely among his people. He

invented the Gothic alphabet, brought the Goths into literary relations with Roman culture, and opened up the pathway for Christian truth into all parts of the Ostrogothic territory. In Greece, it was not Athens, but Corinth, which became the ecclesiastical centre of operations. Athens, however, constituted a diocese, and the third bishop resident there suffered martyrdom A.D. 179. Aquileia, at the head of the Adriatic Sea, became a point of influence for the propagation of Christianity among the peoples of the eastern Alps.

5. **Rome** was the heart and hand of a vigorous and aggressive Christianity. The entire Italian peninsula had grown into episcopates. The first provincial synod was A.D. 303, but before this there had been seventeen smaller synods and councils, attended by bishops of all Italy. Rome converted all Spain and Gaul into a missionary field. The Roman bishop was supreme. As early as the end of the second century Christian societies existed throughout Spain, and by the beginning of the fourth century churches had been established in all the Gallic provinces. Vienne was an episcopal residence, A.D. 118; Lugdunum (Lyons), about A.D. 179; and Treves, in the first half of the fourth century.

6. **Germany.** Christianity was at first communicated to Germany, most likely, by the soldiers in the Roman army. Where colonies were planted, as a provincial centre of Roman authority, the gospel soon acquired a foothold. Colonia (Cologne) became a bishopric about the end of the third century. At the same time the gospel was introduced into Rhætia by the bishop Narcissus. Christianity was also planted far in the north, along the coast of the North Sea. The apostle to Scandinavia was Ansgar, who was born A.D. 801, and whose remarkable triumphs belong to the mediæval period.

7. Britain. It cannot be doubted that the gospel entered Britain at an early period, or about the middle of the second century. Rome, under Julius Cæsar, had conquered the country, and brought it into close relationship with Italy. In the Council of Arles, A.D. 314, three bishops from Britain signed the decrees—Eborius, of Eboracum (York), Restitutus, of Londunum (London), and Colonia Londiniensium (Lincoln). The location of these bishops proves that the whole of England was organized into a complete ecclesiastical system. Succat, the original name of St. Patrick, or Patricius, was born about A.D. 400, of Christian parents, and was originally a slave. He devoted himself to the evangelization of Ireland. Through his influence societies were planted, schools were organized, Christian literature was cultivated, and missionaries went out from that island to the Continent. Columbanus, with twelve companions, went to France, A.D. 580, and began a thorough evangelistic work in the neglected parts of Gaul. Gallus made Gaul the field of his labors. Willibrod, an Englishman, went to Ireland for his Christian education, and then gave his life to missionary labors among the Frisians, along the coast of the North Sea. Boniface, born near Exeter, about A.D. 680, went to Germany and spent his life in that country.

Chapter XXX.

THE CLOSE OF THE EARLY PERIOD.

1. This Rapid Extension of Christianity was the most notable characteristic of the border-land between the early Church and the mediæval period. Missions were promoted by the very growth of the papacy. The bishops saw that their hopes of territorial power could be realized in the West and North rather than in the East, and each strove to surpass his predecessor in the good work. Missionaries and church officers were sent out from Rome with authority to plant missions, build up a literature, and indoctrinate the people in the truths of Christianity. In many instances these attempts failed, the missionaries were killed, and the old heathenism of the provinces triumphed over the young Christianity. But the tide of religious truth was too strong for final resistance. New efforts were made, and finally the old idols were removed, the temples were destroyed, and Christian chapels were erected in their place.

2. Scholarship. Christianity carried with it the disposition to create a literature. The missionary was often a man of ardent theological tastes, and immediately began to adapt the growing literature of Christianity to the new people. Schools, as at Fulda, in Germany, were at once organized. Here the Scriptures were copied, elementary books were written, and small libraries were collected. Centres of theological learning were thus formed. The development of a literary taste was never interrupted, even amid the convulsions of the Middle Ages. The Christian pen and school were never disturbed by the storms of warfare with false faiths.

3. The Venerable Bede represented the patient and scholarly class of his whole age. He was born in Durham, England, about A.D. 673, spent his laborious life of a century at the monastery of Wearmouth and Yarrow, and reared a literary monument of forty different works, twenty-five of which were on Biblical subjects. History and kindred topics were treated in the remaining fifteen. He died in great joy, singing psalms with his pupils, immediately after concluding his Anglo-Saxon translation of John's gospel. Wordsworth, in a beautiful fancy, thus rebukes the idler by presenting the picture of the toiling Bede:

> "But what if one, through grove or flowery mede,
> Indulging thus at will the creeping feet
> Of a voluptuous indolence, should meet
> Thy hovering shade, O Venerable Bede!
> The saint, the scholar, from a circle freed
> Of toil stupendous, in a hallowed seat
> Of learning, where thou heardst the billows beat
> On a wild coast, rough monitors to feed
> Perpetual industry. Sublime Recluse!
> The recreant soul, that dares to shun the debt
> Imposed on human kind, must first forget
> Thy diligence, thy unrelaxing use
> Of a long life; and, in the hour of death,
> The last dear service of thy passing breath."

4. Doctrines. Christian doctrines assumed, by the close of the early period, a settled condition. The Church had elaborated its theological standards, while its creeds were now repeated from the deserts of Africa to the forests of Britain and the shores of the North Sea. The larger heresies had still a constituency, but were in rapid process of disintegration. They throve only in the remoter provinces, more especially in the East, and were alienated from the sympathy of the great body of Christian people in all lands. When the Middle Ages began, other controversies arose, which were largely speculative, and had but little relation to the Arian and other great struggles.

5. Roman Centralization constantly gained strength. Church offices multiplied rapidly, and the close of the early period was the signal for larger measures for Roman primacy. The bishops of Rome were the real rulers of southern Europe, from the Constantinian dynasty to the reign of Charlemagne. The great wealth which had been at the command of the empire was now largely diverted into ecclesiastical channels, and was used to build vast churches, organize missions, support a rapidly growing clergy, found schools, and create a literature.

6. Superstition was the darkest color in the picture of the Church at this transitional period. Miraculous powers were attributed to the overthrow of the dust of the saints. The places where they died were hallowed, and were regarded as most fit sites for stately sacred buildings. The saintly calendar increased rapidly. Festivals were organized in memory of each one who had risen above the surface of his times as an exemplar of piety, devotion, and sacrifice. The condition of the people may account in large measure for the prevalence and force of the tendency towards superstition. When Constantine made Christianity the state religion the many millions of the Roman empire were thrust upon the Church for training and development. The burden was altogether too great. The people of the centres were still beneath the spell of the pagan traditions and gross superstitions which had grown out of polytheistic systems. The populations of the provinces were in even worse plight. Their ancestral faiths were a rude conglomeration of fetichism. There was not even a social elevation on which to build. It is not a matter of wonder, therefore, that when such heterogeneous and untrained multitudes were thrust suddenly upon the Church, for its care, the superstitious habit should be slow to yield to the new Christian conditions. When the Church passed into the darkness of the Middle Ages the question was, could it endure the ordeal of vast wealth, superstition, and clerical assumption? When the Reformation came the question was answered. Much was lost during the long night, but light came at last. The power of the Church to purify itself is the greatest proof of its divine origin, and the clearest prophecy of its certain conquest of the world.

INDEX.

THE END.